Amazon FBA

How to Launch an E-Commerce
Business with Amazon FBA.
A Step by Step Guide to Build a Real
Profitable Business in 2019 and 2020
with the most Popular Online Business
for Beginners.

Jim Work

Table of Contents

Introduction

These days, a lot of emphasis on being placed on the value of being able to work from home and earn money through your computer. For many, online marketing and e-commerce is a powerful opportunity to step out of financial ruin and into a state of financial freedom, with the added benefit of time freedom as well. With the way the economy seems to be going, I suspect that one day everyone will have some form of involvement in e-commerce as a way to subsidize or supplement their income, if not replace their income altogether.

You have likely seen the stories about people who decide to try e-commerce, only to realize that they tapped into a massive revenue stream that has earned those thousands, if not millions, of dollars every single year. From bloggers who have leveraged their websites for an income to individuals who have stepped onto platforms like Amazon, it seems like many have a form of "rags to riches" story that has left the rest of the world in awe.

For many, it also seems like a deal that is simply too good to be true, and that they should not even bother trying because there is no way it could *possibly* work for them.

To those people, I say do your research.

E-commerce is a thriving powerhouse that continues to turn everyday people into individuals who are earning massive amounts of wealth and changing the future of their lives forever. There is no time like the present to get started, which is why I am so excited that you are here right now learning how to navigate the world of Amazon FBA!

Getting started as soon as possible, is key in positioning yourself into the world of e-commerce and earning a piece of the pie for yourself. When you choose to get started with e-commerce, the moment you make the leap you set up the opportunity for your entire future to change. You not only open yourself up to create financial freedom for yourself, but you also set yourself up to receive many other benefits that come with financial freedom being earned through a strategy like e-commerce. For example, you create the opportunity for you to work from anywhere you desire, spend your days doing anything you wish to do, and design the lifestyle that you desire to have for yourself right down to the very last detail. Countless benefits come from the financial freedom and time freedom that you will earn for yourself through launching and managing a successful Amazon FBA business.

The best part is: this business can be built out in a highly passive manner, too. Many people think that you have to have a lot of time and energy to pour into launching an online business, or any business for that matter, in order to see it succeed. However, based on the nature of Amazon FBA and how this program works, you actually step into a form of e-commerce that is easier and more passive than virtually any other form of e-commerce out there. Through this platform, all you have to do is source products, place them for sale, and advertise them to your audience of individuals who are ready to purchase the products from you. Then, all you have to do is let Amazon employees manage the process of actually shipping your products to your customers, while you keep products in stock and source new products to grow your business with.

The concept of Amazon FBA is simple, which is exactly what makes it an incredible business opportunity for those who are new to e-commerce. Instead of having to manage everything from web development to inventory management, shipping and everything else, you simply have to manage marketing while making sure that everything stays in stock. This makes your role in the business wildly easy, meaning that you can grow your Amazon FBA business as a side business, or grow it and let the income sustain your freedom-based lifestyle.

In *Amazon FBA,* we are going to discuss everything you need to know about Amazon FBA, including what it is and how to get started with this business model. By the end of this book, you will be able to confidently design your own Amazon FBA business and grow it to massive success in minimal timing. Through this, you are going to be able to transform your own finances and open yourself up to the opportunity of living your best possible lifestyle.

If you are ready to begin learning the ways of Amazon FBA and preparing to launch your own Amazon FBA business, it is time to begin. Please, enjoy the process. You are about to make some massive, life-changing moves in the coming weeks!

Chapter 1: Amazon FBA in 7 Steps

To help you get an overview of what it is that you are going to be creating, we are going to discuss the seven key steps for creating and growing your Amazon FBA business. Developing an understanding of these seven steps in the first place will help guide you to understand why each step is being taken, and what it is contributing to the greater picture of launching your Amazon FBA business.

Understand that when it comes to launching any sort of business, e-commerce or otherwise, you should always clearly understand why you are doing something. If you do not have a clear understanding for why each step is involved in the process, it is ideal to educate yourself on what that step is and how it contributes to the greater success of your project. When it comes to launching a business or even maintaining a business, everything should always be done intentionally. When you know exactly why you are doing what you are doing, you can ensure that each part of your process is relevant and that you are leveraging that step in the best possible way. In the end, this level of education around what you are doing will prove to be extremely beneficial to your ability to generate the level of success that you desire in your Amazon FBA business, so do not overlook this part in an effort to jump right in and get started. Education and knowledge truly are power in the business world!

Create Your Account
The first step in launching your Amazon FBA business is creating your account. Your Amazon FBA account is the entire basis of your business, as this serves as the main "hub" for everything that you will do with your business. Without it, you will not be able to access anything like Amazon Seller Central, a storefront, or anything else, so it is crucial that you make your Amazon FBA account before anything else.

Because it is designed to serve as the main hub for your business, you want to make sure that every single part of your account is filled out as much as possible. This way, in the matter of using your account for any reason you can feel confident that it has been designed in the best way possible.

When you do set up your account, you want to make sure that you create a professional account and not just an individual account, as Amazon's individual accounts come with a large number of limitations on their uses. Although they are cheaper, they are not the right account for you to open when you start your Amazon FBA account. We will discuss more how you can set up your Amazon FBA account and what you should do while setting up your account in Chapter 2.

Pick Your Product Niche

As you begin to build your Amazon FBA business, you are going to have to pick your product niche, which ultimately identifies what types of products you are going to be selling on your store. When you first launch your Amazon FBA business, you might want to sell virtually everything, especially once you see what the profit margins can be on certain products in various niches. That being said, if you do not pick a clear niche, you are going to have a hard time driving traffic to your storefront because you will not have a clear focus on what exactly it is that you are marketing. These days, when it comes to selling your products, you need to have a clear niche so that you can brand your niche and market it to other people. The strength of your niche is going to be a huge defining factor in your success with Amazon FBA, so do not overlook this part.

Picking a niche requires you to conduct research on which niches are most profitable and which are going to help you create the most success with your business. Once you have picked your niche, every additional part of your business is going to be built around it, so you want to make sure that you are choosing the right niche for your business. We are going to discuss how you can pick a niche in Chapter 3.

Research Your Products

After you have picked your niche, you are going to need to determine what products fit into your niche so that you can identify what it is that you are going to be selling. In chapter 4, we are going to discuss how you can find the best products that fit in your niche and that are going to earn you the best profits from your sales.

When it comes to researching products, there is quite a bit of effort that goes into making sure that you have chosen the right products to sell in your business. With this part of your business, you want to make sure that you are choosing products that are going to earn you the best profit, and that is going to be the most likely to sell. After all, there is no point purchasing product that is not going to earn you a strong profit, or purchasing product that you are going to have to pay lengthy storage fees on overtime, if the product does not sell out very well.

There are many steps involved in researching your products, but they are not hard and should not take any longer than a few sessions researching your products to make sure that you have chosen the best ones possible. It is worthwhile to invest extra time in this part of the process, as doing so will ensure that you are choosing the best products that are going to earn you greater success in your business.

Find Your Suppliers

After you have chosen what type of products you want to sell in your business, you want to search for the suppliers who you are going to purchase these products from. Regarding selling products as a retail business, as you will be with Amazon FBA, you need to source your products from manufacturers or wholesalers who are going to be able to give you the best deals.

Finding the right suppliers for your business is crucial; as they are going to help, you ensure that your products are high quality and that they are shipped to the Amazon warehouses on time. Since your suppliers are going to be responsible for supplying your business with products to sell, you want to make sure that you are working together with suppliers who are going to be easy to work with. It should be easy for you to communicate with your suppliers, easy for you to receive timely and complete answers to your questions, and easy for you to get your products shipped to the Amazon warehouse. You will learn all about how to qualify suppliers and work with them in Chapter 5.

Create Your Brand

You already know what products you are selling and what niche you are selling in, but now you need to start building your brand out. Branding your Amazon store is how you are going to create an impressionable image that can be shared with people during your marketing efforts. Concerning business, your brand is your opportunity to create an identifiable image and reputation that your customers come to know and appreciate. Your brand is the image that you will be building and it is what will earn your business a reputation as being a high quality, and a fun brand to purchase through.

Creating a brand is essential in any business, but especially when you are building on a platform like Amazon, where Amazon already has such a strong brand. If you do not seek to set yourself apart from the rest of the businesses on the platform using strategies like branding, you might find yourself being buried beneath the other sellers who are going the extra mile. With branding, you will not only set yourself apart on Amazon, but you will also be able to build an image and reputation for yourself everywhere else online, too. We will discuss how you can create and leverage your brand in Chapter 6.

Design Your Product Listings

At this point, you will have your products picked out and possibly on their way to Amazon already, and you will have effectively outlined what and whom your brand is. The final step before advertising your products is to create listings for them, so that when people land in your store they see the products that you have available and they are able to purchase them. If your products are not listed in their own listings, you will end up not being able to sell your products because they will not have a purchasing page linked to them.

Creating your product listings is about more than just throwing up a generic description of your product and pointing people to the checkout button, too. With Amazon, the key to creating a strong product listing is to brand the wording that you use in your listing and offering strong pieces of information regarding what the product is, how it is so great, and why people should be purchasing it. We are going to discuss how you can bring all of these elements together into the perfect product listing in Chapter 7, when we discuss how you can launch your new products for sale.

Advertise Your Products

The final step in running a successful Amazon FBA business is advertising your products. At this point, everything is already set up and ready to go and you just need to advertise your products so that people know they are available and ready to purchase. Advertising your products for sale happens both organically (non-paid) and through paid traffic using strategies like social media marketing, paid to advertise, and word of mouth. We are going to discuss everything that you need to know about successfully advertising your Amazon FBA business in Chapters 6 and 8, in order to know how you can acquire traffic through both paid and nonpaid strategies.

Chapter 2: Set Up Amazon FBA

The first step, as you know, is to set up an account with Amazon FBA. Creating your account is the first step because this is where you are going to gain access to everything that you need to launch your Amazon FBA business. With your Amazon account in place, you will have the main hub for your Amazon FBA business fixed in place, so that you are ready to begin selling on Amazon.

What You Need to Know About Amazon Seller Central Account

Your Amazon Seller Central account is the foundation for everything that you do in your business, as you cannot do anything without this account. Although you could complete this step later on after you have already built the rest of your business out, it might not be a great idea, as this will prevent you from acquainting yourself with the platform and learning to navigate it beforehand. Building your account in advance gives you the opportunity to understand none of the features available to you ahead of time, so when considering the time to launch you is attempting to understand a new platform, in addition to managing a launch. As well, many people find that creating the actual account makes their business feel a lot more real, and helps them stay committed to seeing their decision to launch an Amazon FBA business through in a timely fashion.

Amazon Seller Central is going to give you access to everything that you need to know about your Amazon FBA business. Here, you are going to be able to introduce and design your storefront, manage product listings, oversee customer service inquiries, manage your revenue, and gain access to important information such as when stock needs to be reordered and where to send it to. In your account, you will find options to reorder stock and register that stock with Amazon so that they can actually receive your inventory, which is crucial.

Essentially, everything that you will ever need to do regarding the creation, maintenance, or running of your business is going to involve the Amazon Seller Central account in one way or another. The more you can grow comfortable with the platform now, in advance, the easier it is going to be for you to rely on this platform and use it to run your business.

Creating Your Amazon FBA Account

Creating an Amazon FBA account is simple, and does not take more than a few minutes. You will start by going to Amazon's website and scrolling down to the very bottom of the page so that you can see their footer navigation bar. There, you will see a heading that says "Make Money with Us" followed by a link that says, "Sell on Amazon." Click on that link and it will walk you through the systematic process of launching your Amazon Seller Central account.

Right away, you are going to be offered the decision to make an individual account or a professional account. You will notice that the individual account is free, while the professional account is $39.99 per month. Because you are just starting, it may seem tempting to launch a free account, but note that features such as Amazon FBA are not offered to individual account holders, as these accounts are geared more toward selling your own belongings in a "garage sale" type of business. If you want to run a real retail business through Amazon, you need to have a professional account, so you will need to pay the $39.99 fee to launch your account.

After you start your professional account, you will be required to provide information such as who you are, what login credentials you want to use, and what business you are associated with. You may also need to input important information linked to payment and taxes, which will allow Amazon to pay you your profits and offer you a tax slip come tax season. Make sure that you fill out all of this information now, in advance, so that it is ready to go when you begin paid or when it is time for you to declare your taxes at the end of the year.

After you have taken these actions, your Amazon Seller Central account will be created! You will not need to do anything further with your account until you are ready to begin ordering and listing products, at which point you will need the account to complete these parts of the process.

Chapter 3: Skills Needed for Amazon FBA

At this point, your Amazon Seller Central account is launched and you are serious about starting your business. You have made the commitment, and you are ready to get started so that you can start seeing profits come through on the commitment that you have made. Before we really get started, however, I want to get clear on some skills that you are going to need, in order to launch your Amazon FBA and make a passive income through your efforts.

Every single business requires a unique skill set that is going to help you earn an income with that business, and Amazon FBA is no different. Although this platform does not require nearly as many skills for you to succeed, it does require you to have some degree of skills so you should be prepared to understand what these skills are, and continually invest in them in order to generate success.

Building Your Competitive Edge

Although building your competitive edge is a strategy, it can also be considered a skill, as you do grow better at identifying, building, and honing your competitive edge over time. Some people seem to have the strength right off the bat and can identify what helps them stay competitive against the rest of the crowd, and then leverage that competitive edge to succeed right from day one. This is often the case when you identify stories of people who started making tens of thousands, hundreds of thousands, or even millions within their first year of business.

Even if you are not particularly knowledgeable or skilled in this area at first, you can certainly build your skill at being a competitive business owner. The key to identifying and growing your competitive edge knows what makes you more desirable over any other business in your niche. For example, Lulu Lemon is an athletic clothing company based out of Vancouver, British Columbia and it uses its competitive edge of being a local company with high-quality clothes to market to its customers. Apple is a well-known technology company that has the competitive edge of having products that are sleek and that have a modern or futuristic design to them, which they use to appeal to their customers with. Every company that has ever generated any level of success has identified its competitive edge, and then made virtually every single decision in their company based on how they can leverage their competitive edge to maximize their success.

When it comes to being a more competitive business owner as a skill, you will find that the more that you think with the mindset of "what is my competitive edge and how can I leverage it?", the more it comes naturally for you to find these competitive opportunities. As a result, it will become easier for you to create that competitive edge even further and leverage it even more for your business.

Branding Your Business

Much like with finding and leveraging your competitive edge, branding your business is both a strategy and a skill that you have to develop over time. On the issue of seeing your brand as a skill, the easiest way to understand why it is a skill is to recognize that your brand is an identity with its own personality. Even if your brand is based on you, it is going to have its own image, tone of voice, and other elements of it that are based on its own personality rather than yours.

To help you build your skill in branding, you can spend as much time as possible getting to know your brand and to understand what it looks like and who it is. Get to know your brand as if you were getting to know a new friend, and put just as much effort into understanding everything from the more obvious surface-level elements of your brand to the deeper and more meaningful elements of your brand. For example, you might already have a decent comprehension of the fact that your brand is represented by yellow and teal and that you use Arial font types with it, and you might know that it has a more playful and fun tone of voice to it. However, do you know exactly what words your brand would use to speak with your audience in order to share a relatable and impactful message with them? Do you know how and where your brand would incorporate yellow and teal into its imagery to create an image that is not only identifiable but also enjoyable to look at? Do you know how your brand would communicate with customers in private messages to create a professional conversation that still held the tone of your brand?

Knowing these nuances helps you really understand the brand that you are portraying and how you can leverage it to connect with other people. It might take time for you to get to know your brand on this level, but eventually, you will find that the image captions or product descriptions that once took you hours to come up with, eventually only take a few minutes. This is because you can effectively "get into character" as your brand and portray your brand in the best way possible, while still leveraging it to earn sales from your customers.

Tracking and Monitoring Analytics

Your analytics are an important asset to your business as they directly tell you what your customers think about the way that you are doing business. For the most part, your customers are probably not going to go out of their way to message you with feedback on how they feel about your new products, or what they think about your latest marketing techniques, which is why analytics matter. Analytics give you the opportunity to identify what marketing materials are working, which products are the most popular, and what is ultimately causing your customers to purchase from you, or not purchase from you if you are seeing a rut in your sales.

When considering analytics, you are going to need to know how to monitor your analytics directly on Amazon FBA, as they are directly linked to your shoppers and visitors. However, you are also going to want to apply the same skills to your social media marketing strategies, in order to see how your marketing strategies are developing, too. This way, you can feel confident that both your marketing efforts and your shop are performing to the best of their ability, giving you the best chances at earning a sale in your business.

Expense Tracking and Monitoring

In addition to monitoring and tracking your analytics, you also want to monitor and track your expenses related to your business. When you first launch a business, it can be easy to get lost in all of the various purchases that you make to get your business off the ground and get it in front of your audience. From your Amazon Seller Central account fees to advertising fees and product-related fees, your expenses can rack up quickly, and if you are not careful, they can take a toll on your business.

Naturally, when you first launch a business you are going to go into the negatives for a while, as you are going to be spending your own cash on these early purchases. At that point, you will not have any sales, so you will not have made enough profits to make up for the money that you are spending on launching your business. For that reason, you want to be modest in the way that you spend money early on, so that you can quickly earn some revenue and pay back the expenses that you put into launching your business. The sooner that you can break even, the better, as this means you are not out on your own expenses to launch your business.

Just because you want to be modest with your expenses, however, does not mean that you want to be cheap in the way that you are spending your expenses. The idea instead is to consider what expenses are necessary and then purchase the best quality of each product or service that you can reasonably afford. This way, you have a great brand to launch with and you can always upgrade or add more expenses or features later.

After you have launched your business, you are still going to need to pay attention to your expenses and track them effectively. You need to make sure that you are always working toward staying profitable and that you are never spending more than you have or more than you have to, in order to operate your business. Keep your expenses as low as you reasonably can, while still running a quality business, so that you are able to run a great business while also earning an excellent profit.

Investing in Your Marketing Skills

When it comes to Amazon FBA, aside from sourcing and purchasing product and then having them shipped to Amazon, your only other role is to market. With the right marketing skills in place, you can drive huge amounts of traffic to your website and get your products seen. This way, you have higher chances of actually having people purchase your products, which is exactly how you earn your revenue in your business.

As you continue to run your business, you should also continue to work on learning how to grow your marketing skills. Do not be afraid to invest in marketing courses, to take seminars or other learning sessions that can help you learn, and to read about the latest in marketing strategies online. The more that you can keep yourself up to date with how to market, as well as the latest trends in marketing, the more you are going to be able to launch your business with great success.

Eventually, the more successful you grow with marketing the easier it will be for you to get your products in front of customers. This way, you will have an even easier time selling your products because you will be doing and saying all of the right things to get the attention of your audience and to encourage them to look at your shop and possibly purchase your products. Again, the better you get with this, the easier it will be for you to do and the more fluidly you will find yourself earning greater momentum off of each post you make or product you launch.

Chapter 4: Choosing the Right Product

Any retail business, including ones in the e-commerce industry, is only as strong as the products are. When it comes to generating success in your Amazon FBA business, you need to know how to choose the right products for you to sell to your customers so you can earn a strong profit and grow your business consistently over time. At this point, you have a clear understanding of the importance of identifying your competitive edge and you are already consciously and intentionally begun to develop this skillset. Now, you are going to use this understanding to find a product niche that works for you, and to find products that are going to work for your business.

When it comes to picking the right product niche and products for your business, it can be daunting as you realize the importance that this part of your business carries. You might fear that you will make the wrong decision and that you will struggle to generate any success in your business due to a poor choice made at this point. While this can certainly happen, there are plenty of strategies that you can use to help you calculate exactly what niche you should be selling in, and what products you should be selling as a part of that niche. Through using these calculations, you will be able to feel confident that the product niche and products that you choose are going to be profitable and popular enough to help you generate success. While nothing is guaranteed, if you follow these exact steps to verify and validate your product niche and products before committing in any one direction going forward, you will have the greatest odds in your favor.

Identifying Your Product Niche

Regarding identifying your product niche, you want to start by considering what industries you are most passionate about or interested in learning about. Many people underestimate the value of picking a niche that actually interests you, but true marketing masters know that this is the key to find a niche that you are going to be able to grow in. When you are passionate about, or at least interested in a certain subject, you are more likely to invest in learning about it and actually understand what it is that you are learning about. With marketing, this means that you are going to be far more intuitive about what types of trends are ideal for you to partake in, what products are going to succeed in your industry, and how you can grow your business effectively.

After you have identified about 3-5 passions or interests that you could pursue as a business venture, you want to start brainstorming all of the possible products and product lines that you could offer in each niche. Write those potential products or product lines down under each possible niche. In addition to writing down possible product lines, consider areas that you could branch out into as your business grew, too. For example, let us say you wanted to offer graphic t-shirts for women in a product line as your primary product line or the one that you would be starting in. Possible extensions of this could be to add male graphic t-shirts, child graphic t-shirts, and even graphic t-shirts for dogs. Alternatively, you could venture into offering graphic canvas bags, totes, and other female-oriented accessories if you wanted to maintain a female niche.

Getting a clear idea of what you could offer and how you could extend your offers is important, as this is your earliest opportunity to validate that your possible chosen niche would not only be strong in the beginning, but would also have plenty of room for growth. Make sure that you take the time to really consider how these products would fit into your possible niche and whether or not they would make logical sense with your business. It is important that you are honest and concise when you validate possible product niches in order to feel confident that the route you have chosen is going to be a strong one. Now is not the time to be idealistic, but instead to be realistic, as you are going to be placing a lot of weight into this decision and you want to make sure that you minimize the risk as much as possible by validating it as honestly as possible right away.

Next, you need to start narrowing down your possible product niches into ones that are as specific as possible. While you do not want to niche down too hard to the point where you have almost nothing left to offer, you do want to niche down to the point where what you are offering is clear and easily groups together. For example, rather than saying "Gardening supplies" which is too broad or "gardening rakes" which is too specific, you might offer "designer flower pots" as a niche. This way, there are plenty of different product lines that you can incorporate, ranging from modern and sleek to flowery and feminine, yet it is still a clear niche that you are serving.

At this point, you can identify whether or not a niche is ideal based on your level of passion in that niche, the room for growth that it has, and the way that you might be able to narrow it down into a more specific category. All that is left to do is validate your niche with the outside world to ensure that the niche you pick is one that will actually interest other people, which will ensure that you are likely to earn sales from it. Nothing would be more disappointing than validating a niche with yourself, only to launch it to the public and find that it is something that not too many people are interested in.

When it comes to validating your niche, you can do so by researching your chosen niche on platforms like Google Trends. You can also do basic research on social media for your chosen niche by searching up hashtags or keywords relating to your niche and seeing just how popular those terms are. Ideally, you want a niche that has 2-5 million people interested in it so that you have plenty of room for growth. If there is any more than that, you might be attempting to tap into a niche that is far too broad for you to make any level of success in. If you pick one that has a smaller audience, you are not going to have enough people to market to and you will find yourself marketing to no one.

At this point, since you are already researching, it is also a good idea to pay attention to the average price of products in your industry. Knowing this knowledge now will help you get an idea for what price points people are willing to buy the product at, which will help you determine if you are going to have a large enough profit margin to succeed with when you begin to source products for your business.

Discovering Trending and Profitable Products

Now that you have identified your niche, you need to start discovering products that you can sell in your niche that are going to sell quickly and earn you a strong profit along the way! With reference to selling products, there are a few things that you want to be on the lookout for as you choose which products

27

to sell. These particular points are going to ensure that your product makes you the most money in the quickest period, making your business more successful.

When it comes to products that you will be selling online, you want to pick products that are trending, products that are easy to market, and products that are going to have a high-profit margin. You also want to pick products that are going to sell out quickly, as this means that you will not have to spend so much money on storage fees for the products that you are selling. The more that you can stock trending products that sell quickly, the more you are going to earn and the more momentum your store will grow with, which will result in you earning a huge income from your investment.

To begin identifying all of these highly profitable products, you want to start by doing some general product searches. General product searches involve you simply searching your niche on platforms like Amazon, Etsy, and eBay so that you can begin to see what types of products are most common in your chosen niche. Ideally, you want to look for products that retail between $10 to $50, as these are the price points where impulse buys happen, which means that people are going to be likely to make quick purchases on your products. If you price any lower, people will not see it as being worth the investment, and if you invest it any higher people will need to think it over, which will mean it takes them longer to buy the products. In both cases, you are going to be waiting for sales, which will cost you more money and result in you having to work harder to make the sales.

As you do your general search, seek to write down 30-50 products that fall in this price range, including variables and alternatives that people are selling. The more products that you can note down, the better, as this will give you a strong list to pick through when you begin to decide what products you are actually going to sell in your store.

Next, you want to use a tool like Merchant Words or Jungle Scout, which is going to help you identify how strong the market is for products that you are planning on selling. These platforms help you see the exact analytics relating to supply and demand, ensuring that you are getting into a product where the supply exceeds the demand so that you can feel confident that you are going to have people to sell to. Items that are in demand are more likely to sell both at a higher volume, and at a higher speed, which results in you earning a higher profit and in a shorter period. This step should help you narrow your list down by knocking out any products that are not in high enough demand. Especially early on, you do not want to be investing in products that you are going to have to store for lengthy periods because you have chosen something that is not earning cash fast. Instead, you want to pick products that are likely to sell quickly so that you can build momentum and get your business out there, while also quickly earning back the investment that you put into your business.

With what is remaining on your list, you want to turn to Amazon's Best Seller Rankings and begin to identify whether or not your products are ranking well on Amazon itself. Ideally, you want to check out the first three to five products that are on Amazon's Best Seller Ranking's list to see which ones are going to be the most profitable for you in your niche. You can search for different categories that are related to your niche to get each of these products, which will help you validate all of the products that you have chosen to consider for your own business.

The last thing that you need to do when you are searching for products that you want to sell on Amazon FBA is looking at the actual FBA fees. Each type of product is going to have different fees due to it having a different shape, size, weight, storage requirement, and handling requirement than other products. Even products from the same niche will have different needs that will need to be accounted for in the fees, so always consider this before officially investing in the new product. This way, you can identify how much of your profits are going to be sunk into Amazon fees, which will help you determine whether it is worth it or not. For some products, the fees might eat up too much of your profit, leaving the product not worth it for you to truly invest in.

At this point, you should be left with a handful of products that are going to be ideal for you to sell in your store. Do not worry about how many you have identified to sell, unless you have had a hard time finding good products as this may indicate that you have picked too specific of a niche or one that is not strong enough for you to sell in. However, if you find that you have 20-45 products or more on a list of possible purchases, this is a good thing. This proves that there is a strong variety of great products for you to sell and that you will have plenty to grow out into later on.

Validate Your Products through Hands-On Research

Just like with your product niche, you are also going to need to validate your products through actual humans. Understand that just because your niche and product popularity prove positive does not mean that you are going to know how to immediately access the people who are going to be most likely to actually buy your product. If you are not tapping directly into those consumers, you are going to have a hard time getting people to buy from you.

Validating your products through hands-on research allows you to get a feel for where your possible consumers are spending time online and how you can get ahold of them. This way, if you do begin selling that particular product you know exactly where to go to market your product and earn as many sales as possible right off the bat.

The best way to begin validating your audience is by going onto social media platforms and looking up your particular niche on social media. Better yet, search keywords related to your chosen product and get a feel for how many people are talking about that product or using that product in their everyday lives. Ideally, you should see hundreds of thousands of people using those products on each platform that you choose to visit to prove that there is a strong audience for you to market to right away.

As you validate your products this way, make sure that you take note of which keywords and hashtags are turning you up with the best results for where you can find your audience online. Although keeping notes on this information will not be relevant to you right now, it will help you later on when it comes time to market your products, as you will already know where to look to find the people who are most likely to buy them. When you are ready to step into your launch, already having part of the research completed will make the launch process easier for you to do.

Chapter 5: Ordering Product from Suppliers

You now have a list filled with excellent possibilities for products that you could be selling in your shop, which means that you are ready to start sourcing these products so that you can move on to actually selling them! Ordering products tend to be the most daunting part of the entire business, as this is the part where you are taking the biggest risk in your Amazon FBA business. When it comes to ordering products, you are now relying on the idea that these products are going to sell out and you are going to earn a profit from them have sold. If it did not work out in your favor, you could be out a large amount of money and in possession of many products that you do not want to have any longer.

Fortunately, if you conducted the research properly in the last chapter, your list should be filled with great products that are virtually guaranteed to sell, so long as you continue to follow the rest of the steps outlined in this book. This means that at least some of the stress should be taken off and that you can start settling into the idea that you are going to be successful, because you are using a winning guideline for how you can earn money using Amazon FBA.

In this chapter, you are going to go through important series of finding suppliers and qualifying them for your business. You are also going to learn about how you can place your order, and when it is the right time to pull the trigger on placing your order. This way, you can feel confident that you have ordered your products properly and at the right time.

Selecting Possible Suppliers for Amazon FBA

The first thing that you need to do is create a list of possible suppliers that you might consider for stocking your Amazon FBA shop with. At this point, you can easily begin to identify possible suppliers by doing a Google search on suppliers who offer a particular product that you are looking for. When it comes to looking for suppliers you want to look at both wholesalers and manufacturers, as both are going to be able to offer the services that you need to stock your Amazon FBA shop. Avoid shopping through other retailers as their markups are going to be excessive for this particular purpose, since their products are priced for consumers and not businesses who want to purchase large quantities.

As you look for suppliers, be sure to jot down possible suppliers next to every single product that you are considering selling in your store. This way, you can have access to their information for reference when you begin to qualify the suppliers, which will make it easier for you to compare them against one another and validate their quality. Ideally, you want to have 2-3 suppliers per product variety to ensure that you are going to have plenty to choose from. If you have only one, you can still jot it down, but it may not measure up during the qualifying process, which means that you may have a lower chance of stocking that particular item unless your possible supplier is high quality.

After you have found all of the possible suppliers who can help you stock your shop, you want to start writing down important information about each supplier. Think of all of the information that would be relevant to you purchasing their products, and use that to help you create comparison charts. You want to consider how expensive their products are, what their minimum order quantity is, how expensive shipping is, how long it takes for their products to arrive after being shipped, and how they handle quality control complaints. You also want to consider where they are located, as this might contribute to how easy or difficult they are to communicate with. If a company is located overseas, it may indicate that they will be more challenging to communicate with due to the language and cultural barriers that you both face. That being said, overseas companies do tend to produce cheaper goods, so consider the quality of the written content on their website to identify how easy they are to interpret. If their written content is incredibly low or poorly translated, it may indicate that they are going to be harder to communicate with and that you might run into troubles with communication. If their written content seems easy to interpret and well written, chances are they will be easier to communicate with which will make your job easier when you choose to work with them.

With your comparison charts completed, take a moment to disqualify obvious non-contenders. This means any company who is going to be too expensive to shop through, any company with low-quality shipping services, or any company who might be too challenging to communicate with should be disqualified. At this point, there is no reason to further research these particular companies as possible suppliers, if you can already tell that they are not offering what you are looking for.

Qualifying Suppliers and Their Products

Any suppliers that have made it past the obvious disqualifications on your comparison charts are now ready to enter the qualifying stage. This is where you are going to qualify both suppliers and their products to determine which company is going to offer the highest quality of products and services for what you are looking for. This part of the process can be lengthy as you are going to be researching and testing several different companies to ensure that the products that you are going to be stocking are high quality and are coming from great suppliers.

The first step in qualifying a supplier is to make contact with them. As you make contact with the supplier, message them to let them know that you are interested in considering their products for your shop. You can also ask questions such as how long shipping typically takes, what shipping methods they use, how early you should order products when you need to restock, and what their minimum quantity orders are. Even if these types of questions are already answered on the website, make sure to ask them in the email as well. In doing so, you gain the opportunity to see how well they communicate and whether or not they offer positive service when you are inquiring about doing business with them. At this point, some suppliers might take a long time answering, or they might answer in a way that is difficult to understand or that suggests that there will be great difficulty in overcoming language or cultural barriers when you are purchasing with them. This does not mean that they are a bad supplier, but it does mean that you might have difficulty communicating with them to deal with any possible needs or issues that you may face along the way.

Once you have received information back from a possible supplier and you have scored the quality of service and communication that they have offered, you want to move on to ordering samples from them. Ideally, you should order one sample of every single product that you are considering buying from them, so that you can get a hands-on feel for the quality of that product. This is your primary opportunity to engage in quality control on the physical products that you are considering selling, so it is incredibly important. Do not rely on reviews and probability here: *always test the product.* If you do not, you might risk having a low-quality product for sale that could do great damage to your reputation as well as cost you significantly in returned orders or inability to move product. *Do not skip this step.*

At this point, you have effectively established a personal opinion on suppliers and you have validated the quality of their products. The last step before committing to a supplier is doing additional research to see what you can learn about that supplier. Remember: sometimes, salespeople will do and say; everything they need to in order to get you to purchase from them, but then the quality of service goes downhill from there. This does not mean that everyone will do this, but some businesses are guilty of it and if you are caught in this, it can leave you in a huge deficit with your products. The best way to avoid this is to look for external evidence that the supplier you have chosen is going to be able to offer high-quality products and service. You can do this by looking for external reviews on their company, which can be done by either Googling their company for reviews, or by joining social media groups and online forums devoted to e-commerce. In these areas, you can find reviews by real people who have actually worked with that particular company to see what the truth is about that particular company. This way, you can identify any possible issues beforehand in order to avoid being caught in an unwanted situation with expensive products on hand.

When and How to Place Your Order

You should now feel confident in who are planning to order your products from, and which products you are going to be stocking your store with for your launch. Now, you need to know how to determine when you should place your order and what needs to happen for your order to be placed. When it comes to Amazon FBA, the way that orders are placed are slightly different and do require more steps, so be sure to pay close attention to this part to ensure that you are following the steps correctly. Doing this incorrectly could lead to an expensive mistake where Amazon ships your products back to the supplier because they were not properly registered, which you would then have to pay for. You would also have to pay again for your products to be shipped back to Amazon, which could result in three possible charges as opposed to one, which can be incredibly expensive on large shipments of stock.

The first thing you need to understand is that you do not have to order your products right away. In fact, you should not order your products just yet, as you will want to have some form of brand and audience in place before you begin launching products, therefore you have people to market your products to. So, until you begin engaging in organic social media marketing and building a small name for your brand, do not order products just yet. This proactive marketing is a crucial first step for eCommerce businesses as this is how you establish your earliest crowd and begin to guarantee your earliest success. Ideally, you should have 500-1,000 people in your social media audience on your chosen primary platform before you begin to actually release products to anyone. This way, you have a strong, healthy audience filled with people who have already shown interest in the types of products that you are going to have available.

After you have an existing audience to launch to, you can submit your orders for your chosen products and start having them

37

shipped to Amazon's warehouse. This way, you have your products ready to go for the launch date and you officially move your project into motion. At this point, you are making your launch a real thing and you are reaching the point of no return.

With ordering your products, you are going to have to fulfill your supplier's requirements and fulfill Amazon's requirements in order to purchase your products, and have them shipped to and accepted by Amazon's employees. You should start by approving your products in the Amazon backend, so that when you order your products from the manufacturer Amazon already approves them.

You can have your products approved on Amazon by signing into your Amazon Seller Central account and going to "Manage Inventory." There, you want to select "New Inventory" and then fill out all of the details about the new products that you are going to be stocking that will be sent to Amazon. What information is needed will depend on what types of products you are sending, so the best guidance to follow here is everything that you see on screen. Make sure that everything Amazon requests are filled out to the best of your ability. Be especially careful in uploading product SKUs into your product profile, as Amazon will deny any products that do not have the exact SKU that you have uploaded so despite tiny inaccuracy can turn out to be disastrous.

After you have registered your new product into your Amazon Seller Central account, you can go to your Manage Inventory page once again, highlight the chosen product, and click "Action on Selected" and then click "Send/Replenish Inventory." You will then be prompted to create a new shipping plan for the product that you are going to be shipping to the Amazon warehouse, so that Amazon's employees know what is happening with your shipment.

The first step in creating your shipping plan is confirming the ship-from address, which is the address of your supplier that will be shipping the products to Amazon. Make sure that you get this address correct because if there are any troubles with your shipment, Amazon is going to send it back to the manufacturer, and if the address is wrong, this could get even more expensive with a lost package.

Next, you need to confirm your packing type. Amazon offers two options to choose from individually packed or case packed. If you are going to be selling individual items, you are going to select individually packed as your packing type. If you are going to be selling multiples grouped together, you want to select case packed. For example, if you were going to sell one individual box of tea, you would select individually packed. However, if you were going to sell ten individual boxes of tea together as a case, you would select case packed. It is worth mentioning that if you are selling individual packages or cases; make sure to mention this to your suppliers so that they can package your products properly for Amazon.

With this information inputted, your basic shipping plan will be designed and now you will have to create the rest of the shipping plan for your package. You will click "Continue to Shipping Plan" and then you will need to select the preparation method. Either you can prepare a shipping plan yourself, or you can request that Amazon creates the shipping plan for you.

Then, you need to prepare and label your products, which will all be done through the systematic system built into Amazon FBA's platform. Next, you will set the quantity and print those labels as needed. Finally, you will preview your shipment, prepare your shipment, choose your shipment type, and then confirm your shipment.

Regarding choosing your shipment type there are two options: Small Parcel Delivery, or Less Than Truckload. Small Parcel Delivery would be anything coming in a single box. For this, you would input the weight and dimensions of each box and put that into your pack list. If you choose Less Than Truckload, this means you are getting a large number of boxes delivered, so you will need to indicate the number of boxes being delivered and enter all of the shipping information from your carrier into them.

Once you have confirmed all of this through Amazon FBA, you can confirm and finalize your order through your supplier. At this point, all you should need to do is purchase the quantity from your supplier and give them Amazon's warehouse address, which can be found in the information with your shipping plan. Then, your products should be shipped to Amazon and they should be managed according to your shipping plans instructions. Information about your shipment will be uploaded directly into your Amazon Seller Central account, where you will be able to see if the shipment has been received and how much stock you have with each product. At first, you should have the entire stock that you ordered, however as it begins to sell you will start seeing those numbers drop.

Chapter 6: Selling Products

Aside from ordering and stocking products for Amazon to ship to your customers, the other part of your Amazon FBA business that you need to oversee is marketing and selling. When it comes to launching your Amazon FBA business, this is one of the biggest elements as your marketing efforts can either make or break your success with your business. A strong marketing plan will get lots of traffic onto your website and will have many people purchasing the products that you are stocking, whereas a weak marketing plan will struggle to get anyone to even pay attention to your brand, never mind your products.

Marketing and sales go hand in hand, as a strong marketing strategy will sell your products for you. If you have a strong marketing plan put together, people will already be prepared to buy your products before they even land in your Amazon FBA store, which means that the sale is already complete. This type of high-quality traffic can be guaranteed by educating yourself on how marketing and branding work, and then applying those techniques into your own business strategy.

In this chapter, we are going to discuss how you can create a strong brand, how you can create a marketing and sales funnel to drive traffic to your website, and how you can leverage organic marketing strategies, such as SEO, to grow your business. Take your time to understand these strategies and to educate yourself, as this is where you have your biggest opportunity to sell products within your business. I will note where you can focus your research on for future learning, so that you know which topics are most important for you to continue learning about, as you become an even stronger marketer and entrepreneur.

Creating a Strong Brand

If you want to create a powerful marketing strategy, you need to have a strong foundation to carry you forward. The foundation of any marketing strategy lies in the brand that is being marketed in the first place, as your brand provides you with a core image and key guidelines to help you decide how to establish your presence and market your business. This is one area where many Amazon FBA business owners go wrong: they believe that Amazon is already branded and therefore they do not need to brand their own business because it has already been done. The fact of the matter is, Amazon has branded Amazon, which means that you and every other seller that is selling on the platform are all being leveraged as the brand. The sellers on Amazon who are taking the time to stand out and improve their own image, while driving massive amounts of traffic to the platform, are the sellers that are going to be favored by Amazon's platform and offered better rankings and traffic from the platform itself.

If you want to be one of Amazon's preferred sellers who earned the best rankings and the best positions in search results, you need to put in the effort to brand yourself and drive your own traffic to your store, too. This way, Amazon sees your business as being a popular one and helps improve your traffic by driving some of its own traffic to you, too. This is all a part of the Amazon algorithm, which you will learn more about later in this chapter.

Creating your own brand defines who you are, what you have to offer, and why people should choose to shop with you over any other brand out there. You can design your own brand with minimal effort and leverage this image and personality to get your brand in front of a larger audience. All you need to do is determine who your target audience is, create an image that suits your brand, and create a tone that determines how your brand is going to sound in all marketing efforts. With these three elements in place, you will have plenty to launch a strong, marketable brand that will help you grow your Amazon FBA business much faster.

Identifying your target audience is a crucial step in the brand building because it allows you to know how you can create a brand that is going to appeal to your audience. Different demographics have different desires when it comes to how brands look and sound, so you are going to want to cater one specifically to your demographic. You can easily find out whom your target audience is by considering what your product niche is, and then determining who is the most likely person to buy that particular product. That person is your target audience. When you identify that person, make sure that you identify them clearly. Understand who they are, where they come from, what their income level is, where they spend time online, and what they are doing with their spare time. The more that you can understand your target audience, the more you can connect with them and create relatable branding and marketing materials that are going to be far more likely to attract your target audience to your business.

The next part of your business is your imagery. This includes your brand colors, your logo, and the general image that you are giving off for your brand. On the issue of choosing your brand colors, look at your competitors and see what types of color palettes they have been using, as this will give you an idea as to what types of colors are popular in your industry. Unbelievably, color preferences do vary by demographics so you are going to want to pick a color palette that fits the pattern for what already exists in the industry. This does not mean that you should be directly copying your competitors, but it will help give you an idea as to what colors are going to work best for you and your business.

Logos are easy to purchase, especially with platforms like Fiverr. For your Amazon FBA account, you can easily hire someone for $40-$250 and have your logo made for your business. This logo is going to be displayed on everything to help people develop brand recognition and know what belongs to your business, so make sure that it is a brand that you are going to enjoy. There are many different styles of logos, so once again choose one that fits your industry well.

Lastly, you are going to need to pick the general image of your brand. That is: what feel do you want to give off with your marketing materials? Are you wanting people to feel connected and like they have a sense of community around them, or are you wanting people to feel like they are independent and empowered? Do you want people to feel fun and inspired, or do you want them to feel serious and important? Consider what you are selling and what mood fits your niche, and then design your brand image around that. For this, you want to pick your chosen brand fonts and the actual content that you will be featuring in your images.

When it comes to designing the imagery for your brand, a popular tool that marketers use is known as a "mood board." Mood boards are graphics that feature the ideal image and mood that a brand will be portraying with their business. This includes their logo, their chosen brand colors, their fonts, and graphics that portray their ideal mood or feel based on what they want customers to feel when they shop with them. You can easily create a board like this using a platform like Pinterest or Photoshop. Once you have it, keep it nearby and then gauge every piece of marketing material against your board to make sure that it has the right feel for what you are going for with your business.

The last part of building your brand is creating the tone or the voice of your brand. Creating the tone or the voice of your brand includes identifying what you want your brand to sound like and then identifying what vocabulary would match that sound. For example, if you want your brand to come across as fun you might use words like flair, whimsical, and entertaining in your marketing content. If you want your brand to come across as serious, however, you might use words like sleek, empowering, and modern.

Again, how you choose your brand voice relies heavily on whom you are talking to, as you want to create a brand that is going to be relatable to your audience. Consider your brand as its own entity and your audience as your brand's friends. Your audience is only going to befriend your brand if they feel a sense of connection to what you are offering them, so you need to make sure that you are offering something relatable. The easiest way to pick your tone is to identify what successful businesses in your niche are using and use that same tone. This way, you can feel confident that you are going to have a sound that is relatable and that is proven in your industry.

The one key difference when you are building a brand is creating your uniqueness. You do not want to sound the same as every other brand any more than a person wants to have six of the exact same friends. You need to identify your unique vocabulary and way of speaking that belongs to you and that sets you apart from everyone else in the room. Remember, you want to be a *friend,* not a *clone.* Choose a way to speak that feels more relevant to your brand and individualized to who you are, yet still relatable to your audience and this will help you market your brand effectively.

Building Your Marketing and Sales Funnel

After you have built your brand, you want to build a marketing and sales funnel. Many who are new to business view sales funnels as being unimportant or only relevant for passive income streams, but the truth is that every single brand needs sales to funnel. The purpose of a sales funnel is to drive traffic to your website so that people can purchase your products. This can be as passive or active as you desire to be, and it can be as simple or strategic as you desire it to be, too.

Ideally, a sales funnel should get your audience to a checkout link in three clicks or less. That being said, you can have many different entry points where people enter your sales funnel so that they can get into the process of getting into those three clicks or less cycle. For example, you might bring people into your sales funnel through paid advertisements, organic social media content, and word of mouth. Then, once they are in that funnel, they are exposed to your business and are directed to your shop and then the checkout page so that they can purchase from your business.

When you first start out in business, it is useful to keep your sales funnel and a number of entry points as simple as possible so that you do not become overwhelmed. Once you begin to feel confident in those entry points and funnels, you can begin to branch out into other ones, allowing you to send even more traffic to your website. The key here is to leverage your momentum and maximize your sales by consistently growing at a pace that you can reasonably manage. If you attempt to grow faster than you can manage, you are going to crash fast and hard and you are going to completely blow up your entire business.

The easiest way to create a sales funnel is to identify one entry point, identify how that entry point can lead to interest, and identify how that interest can lead to a sale. Below I will outline some great sales funnels that you can consider using as your initial sales funnels while you start to grow your business.

- Paid Advertisement > Customer Clicks Advertisement > Product Sales Page
- Social Media Post > Customer Clicks Website Link > Product Sales Page
- Email Newsletter > Customer Clicks Website Link > Product Sales Page
- Lands on Social Media Page > Messages Shop > Product Sales Page Link Offered
- Blog Post > Customer Clicks Link in Post > Product Sales Page

Although some sales funnels get much more complex with various steps that cause customers to sign up for email newsletters, purchase small "tripwire" purchases, and then purchase larger products, not all sales funnels need to work this way. In fact, early on, the easier your sales funnel is, the better will be. When you have a simple sales funnel, it is easy for you to manage and drive traffic through, and it is easy for you to troubleshoot if something in the sales funnels stops working.

Over time, if you desire, you can begin to automate new features into the sales funnel, however, it is not necessary.

The idea with Amazon FBA is that everything is as simplified as possible. Your primary goal is to drive people to your product pages so that they can fall in love with your product and purchase it. At most, an Amazon FBA sales funnel should be 4 steps long in order to feature an email newsletter sign up before a person is lead to the product page. This way, you have your email list growing which gives you direct access to your existing audience anytime you need it. You can easily capture emails using a simple landing page with a platform like MailChimp, Squarespace, or even Shopify.

Understanding the Amazon Algorithm

Every single platform that you might browse or sell on features an algorithm. The algorithm is a term that describes and identifies the way that a company organizes its posts or products for people who are searching their platform. This way, the platform can feel confident that it is showing content that is most relevant to the individual who is shopping on their page, which means that they are more likely to stick around. Most algorithms strive to provide relevant, high-quality content for their viewers so that they feel as though they are seeing exactly what they want to see when they land on the page. This way, they are more likely to stick around and continue browsing. Amazon's algorithm is no different.

When it comes to understanding Amazon's algorithm, your key reasoning is to identify how you can improve your search rankings so that you can be viewed higher up in the results pages. The better your search rankings are, the closer to the top you will appear. According to a recent study, more than 70% of Amazon's shoppers will never click past the first page when it comes to finding what they want to buy, and 35% of them will click on the first product that appears on the first page. The first three products on the entire page will receive 64% of total clicks, making them the most popular and most likely to be purchased products. Clearly, you need to make it a priority to get your products into these top rankings so that you will be more likely to earn sales from your Amazon FBA business.

Amazon is currently using what they call their "A9 algorithm." According to professional marketers, A9 is easier to understand than even Google's algorithm, which means that it should not be terribly hard for you to figure it out even if you are brand new to this. A9 is influenced by text match relevancy, availability of stock, and price.

Regarding text match relevancy, Amazon wants to make sure that they are going to show products that are actually relevant to what the individual is looking for. This way, they can feel confident that if a customer looks up "Laptop Case" they do not receive results like "phone case" or "briefcase", but that they actually see listings of laptop cases. You can improve your own text match results by making sure that your descriptions are clear and concise and that you do not use any words that might falsely advertise what it is that you are selling. This way, when you show up on search rankings, your product is relevant and you are more likely to get clicks from people who are searching for products just like yours.

Availability of stock is important because if you run out of stock you are going to lose your place in the algorithm. Furthermore, if you lose your placing you will not be instantly placed back toward the top of search rankings when you restock, you are going to have to refill your stock and then regain your ranking once again. For this reason, it is important that you always keep your products in stock so that you can maintain your excellent rankings.

Lastly, you need to have competitive pricing. Although it is okay to have a product that is priced higher than others, if you are priced too high your competitors are going to receive more traffic than you are. Amazon wants to be known for offering its customers the best deals, so promoting a store that is overpricing their products is not high on its list of things to do. If Amazon were to do this regularly, they would lose their reputation of being competitively priced and this would damage their own brand image. If you want to improve your search rankings, you need to price competitively so that you are more likely to be viewed over anyone else.

Optimizing Your Products with SEO

For the last section of this chapter, we are going to discuss how you can optimize your products using SEO (search engine optimization) strategies so that you are more likely to be seen by your target audience. Optimizing your products with SEO helps you leverage the algorithms natural search parameters so that Amazon sees you as being an excellent fit for their inquiring customers, meaning that you are more likely to be seen than anyone else.

The first step in optimizing your product listing for SEO is in the title that you use for your products. The title is the first thing that your potential buyer is going to see, so it needs to be relevant and to-the-point so that viewers immediately know what they are looking at and what they can expect from you. Many sellers have a tendency to title their products wrong by attempting to make it sound catchy or interesting, which wastes word count and actually works against them in the algorithm. The more direct you are the better will be. The best way to title your products is to use the following ordering for your information: brand, product line, packaging quantity, material, product type, color, additional information. For example, one product is titled: "MSRM Wand Portable Document & Image Scanner/USB Mobile Scanner Include 8G Micro SD Card and Battery [Silver]." This might sound like a mouthful, but it is actually a great title that tells the customer everything they need to know before they even land on the page. Furthermore, it helps Amazon know that you are relevant to what they are searching and produce you as a high-ranking item in search results.

Next, you need to include some keywords in your copy. Before you start writing your product description, you can find keywords that are relevant to what your audience is actually looking for. The best way to find keywords is to look at your most successful competitors and notice what keywords they are using to describe what their products are. You can easily do this by browsing over three items from your top three competitors in your chosen product category and then identifying what their keywords are. After you have identified all of the keywords, you can remove any that are not relevant and use the rest in your own product description. Make sure that in doing so you create a product description that is relevant and that actually describes what the product is that the individual is looking at. Simply listing keywords in your product description is going to have your product viewed as spam and will massively destroy your ranking on Amazon, as Amazon's algorithm, in particular, is incredibly sensitive toward spam content.

When it comes to creating product descriptions, bullet points have been reported as being important in helping to improve conversion ratios. Using bullet points in your product descriptions and putting important blurbs of information in those bullet points helps naturally draw the eye through the sales page. This result in people having an easier time reading the description and getting to the important information that they actually want to know about. This also results in more people purchasing the product because they see the information that they want and need to see in order to validate and complete the sale.

Another factor that contributes greatly to your ranking is how many people are actually buying your product. The more people that you can get to land on your page and buy the product from you, the better you are going to rank on Amazon. This means that the more you can drive your own traffic to your pages and have those individuals actually buy your products, the more traffic you are going to receive organically through Amazon because the higher you will rank. This is a large reason as to why it is so important to put your own efforts into branding and driving traffic to your business from elsewhere: because it not only leads to you receiving more traffic from other platforms, but it also builds your organic traffic, too.

As you create your product listings, make sure to use high-quality images that clearly show what an individual is going to be purchasing from you. Make sure that your images are in higher pixels and that they clearly display what the product is with clean, bright lighting, and an obvious focus on the product being sold. This way, when a person lands on your listing they know exactly what you are selling and they can easily see it and zoom in, if they feel the need to. With higher quality images, you improve people's likelihood of choosing your page over anyone else's, which implies that you have a higher likelihood of making the sale, too. As you take images, also consider the customer experience during the process in order to get high-quality images that are relevant to what the customer actually wants to see. Merchants have reported that offering 360-degree rotating images, multiple views at different angles, and images with real faces in the artist feature when they are selling artwork, has all improved their results in landing more customers through their listings.

Finally, Amazon Enhanced Brand Content is a feature that allows brands to create branded graphics and flyer-type documents for their products filled with plenty of relevant information for their products. Using these Enhanced Brand Content pieces not only helps people modify and strengthen their description fields, but it is also said to improve your search rankings in the algorithm. If you want to grow on Amazon, using Enhanced Branded Content is an excellent approach.

Chapter 7: How to Launch your Products

When it comes to launching a business, how you launch your products is crucial. Product launches give you the opportunity to build up momentum in your business by generating excitement around a new product that you are going to be releasing, which helps you sell larger volumes of that particular product much faster. If you skip the launch process, you end up launching new products or product lines into an audience that was completely unaware that anything new was coming in the first place. This means that your audience was not prepared with enough excitement, or sometimes cash, to actually purchase your new products, which means it, will take longer for your product to sell.

A sometimes-frustrating reality for new product lineups is that if you do not gain enough momentum from the start, you may never actually gain enough traction to consistently sell that particular product. Product launches gain momentum for the initial sales, then give you the reviews and buzz that you need to continue making sales to additional customers who were waiting to see how the initial launch went. Just a few strategic products launch early on can build a significant buzz around your business, which leads to consistent increasing success every time you launch an additional product afterward. This is a great opportunity for you to massively grow your business as rapidly as possible and, in fact, it is the secret to any great product launch that leads to a business achieving what appears to be an overnight success to other outside businesses.

A Simple Launch Blueprint

Regarding launching your new products, a simple blueprint that you can follow will help you build a successful launch every single time. This blueprint helps you create a strong marketing strategy for your new products that are backed with analytics and evidence to prove that your product is going to reach the eyes of the right customers every single time. The more that you follow this exact blueprint, the easier it will be for you to launch your products and over time it will become effortless for you to launch. As a result, you will find that each subsequent product launch becomes even easier and more successful, making it effortless for you to get your products in front of your audience.

The first step in any launch strategy is identifying which part of your audience you are talking to. On one level, you are going to be talking to your entire audience, since you have already identified a product niche with a specific group of people who are going to be interested in your niche. On another level, each product has a more specific target audience that is going to be interested in exactly what you have to offer. For example, let us say you did go with the designer flowerpots business plan. In this case, if you were to launch a floral feminine flowerpot line, you might find that you are more likely to reach women around 30-40 years old with that product line. Alternatively, if you were to launch a lineup of flowerpots that were more sleek and modern, you would be more likely to reach men or women around 20-35 who were into urban living styles. Identifying exactly which part of your audience is going to be most interested in your current product line is imperative, as this is how you are going to speak directly to those individuals in your audience.

After you have identified which part of your audience is going to be the most likely to purchase your new products, you need to begin creating marketing materials that speak directly to that particular segment of your audience. This means that you need to identify what trends they are interested in, what hashtags they are using, and what vocabulary they are using to speak with each other at the time of you preparing to release your products. Understand that language and trends evolve rapidly so you are going to need to conduct this basic research every single time you begin to release a new product.

Next, you need to know why your audience is going to be interested in purchasing the new products that you have to offer. What problem are you solving, or what need or desire are you fulfilling with your product that makes your audience interested in purchasing it in the first place? Creating a deeper understanding of why your audience would be interested in buying your product in the first place will help you create marketing materials that get your product in front of your audience with a distinct reason for why they should buy it.

When this is done, you want to start marketing your new product to your audience. Remember: the key here is momentum, so you want to build as much momentum around this new product as you possibly can. You want to start by creating curiosity and intrigue in what you are offering with pieces of marketing material that hint that something brand new is coming to your store, and soon. Spend at least a week or so building up suspense around the fact that there is a secret taking place, or getting people interested in learning about what your new products are going to be. Do not be afraid to leave hints and little pieces of information that clue your audience in to what the product might be, and who might be the most interested in purchasing it. Say something like: "who loves floral decorations? We do! We'll bet you love our brand new product being released (date)..."

At this point, as soon as interest begins building in your products, you need to announce what you are offering and start getting your customers excited about it through actually seeing what it is. If you attempt to string them along too long, you might end up losing their interest, as they grow bored of trying to discover what your new product is going to be. You can avoid and overcome this by announcing your product just a week or so after, you begin to build interest in it through sharing clues and hints about your product.

Now, you want to market your new product for a week or two, possibly up to four weeks depending on the size of the launch that you are doing. If you are launching just one or two new products, you want to keep the length of your launch shorter as this will help you maintain momentum. With fewer products, you do not have as much to talk about, in the sense that you will run out of new and interesting things to say if you launch your products over too long of a period. If you are launching a whole lineup, such as through launching a brand new store, you want to give yourself about a month to build up momentum and excitement around your new release. This way, you have plenty to talk about leading up to your official launch date, which makes it the perfect type of launch to span out over a longer period.

Over the period of your launch, you want to share new pictures and updates about the products and any information pertaining to the products that might spark interest with your customers. Talk about the features, the design, and the color options, why it is better than any other product out there and anything else that you can think of that makes the product worthy of the investment. You should also get people thinking about how they can incorporate the product into their own lives by talking about how they could be using it in their everyday lives or how it could be enhancing their quality of lives as they go.

Over the days leading up to the launch you should be posting four or five times per week, and up to once per day, on each social media platform that you are engaged with. Come launch day, you can post 2-3 times per social media platform so that you can get your name in front of your audience and remind them about the big event that is happening that day.

After launch has happened, there will be certain follow-up strategies that you will want to enforce, in order to help you keep the momentum of your launch going, allowing you to continue selling products even long after your initial launch day. This way, you can keep the momentum of your launch going until it comes time for you to release another product or product line with your business.

Before Your Launch

Now that you have the launch blueprint outlined, we are going to break down each part of the launch into three steps: before, during, and after your launch. This way, you can find out exactly what you need to be doing in order to test and prepare your audience for the launch that is yet to come, as well as make plenty of sales on day one and several more on the days following your launch.

Before you begin any launch strategies, you need to outline what the actual strategy itself is going to be. This is your opportunity to organize what needs to be done throughout your launch, so that each day of your launch strategy you know exactly what you need to be doing and how it is contributing to the bigger picture. Just as with other elements of your business, you want to make sure that you know exactly what each part of the process is for in order to maximize its efficiency and make the best launch strategy possible.

As outlined in the launch blueprint, the first part of your launch strategy is going to be identifying the key informational pieces about your launch, such as who you are launching to, why you are launching to them, and why they should buy your product. Finding out this information in advance will help you outline a marketing strategy that clearly markets to your ideal audience and helps you get the most sales possible.

At this point, you should already know what products you are launching, so the next part is finding out which exact part of your audience is going to be the most interest in this product. You can find this information out by looking at your competitors and finding out that exact demographics are purchasing similar products from them. Then, start looking at your own audience and identifying where that demographic lies and how you can reach them within your business. This is a crucial step as you are going to spend the next few weeks talking to this part of your audience, so you need to know whom they are and what you are saying to them to ensure that you are saying something that is likely to get paid attention to.

As you continue to research your audience, take the time to understand who they are and what their behaviors are. Get to know where they like to spend their time online, what they are doing there, and how they are interpreting the content that they are already seeing in these places. Then, begin to create a strategy for how you can talk to your audience including what you are going to say, and when, to reach them and actually be heard by them, too.

Once you have identified who you are talking to and what you are going to say, the next part of your launch strategy is to outline what you are going to say and when. This part of your launch strategy is directly linked to marketing, as it helps you identify exactly what you are going to be posting on each day leading up to your launch. You do not have to be intensely specific about each post that you will be making, but it should fairly clearly outline what the purpose of that post is and what type of content you are going to be sharing on those days.

Some examples of content that you might want to share during your launch include:
- The day that the launch will take place
- What product is being launched
- Why the product is superior
- Why you are so excited about this particular product
- How this product can fit into day to day life
- How much longer is left until the launch
- Varieties of the products that will be available
- Customization features that may be offered
- Samples of other people using the products

As you share your posts, be sure to focus on one specific aspect of it every single time. This way, you have plenty to talk about, rather than giving away all of the information in one long post.

When it comes to social media, people are less likely to read the long posts and they are less likely to read any future posts if they have already grown bored from your original lengthy post. Rather than putting it all out there at once and missing the opportunity to build momentum and interest, you want to break it up into smaller posts and share them over several days, which makes your audience more likely to read what you have to say, and builds excitement.

You should outline a general guide for what you are going to talk on each social media platform each day, leading up to the launch so that you know what you will be posting, when, and where. As you create this guideline, you should also outline what keywords and hashtags you are going to be using to help you leverage algorithms and get your posts higher up in the newsfeeds of your followers. Having hashtag pods and keywords researched in advance makes writing your content a breeze throughout your launch. Remember: the more you prepare for your launch, the less stressful it will be once you begin your launch process, which means that you will be more likely to build the momentum that you need to generate success with your launch.

During Your Launch

After you have organized your launch plan, your primary goal is to stick to your plan as closely as possible. You should have already outlined when you are going to start the launch and when you are going to post or talk about the launch, so at this point, all you need to do is follow these steps to begin sharing and talking about your products.

Aside from following your strategy, you want to pay attention to your analytics throughout the launch process as they are going to give you clear insight, as to how each piece of marketing material is working toward building momentum with your launch. Each time you launch a piece of material, pay attention to the analytics immediately after the post has launched, an hour after, a few hours later, a day later and two days later. These are excellent periods for you to pay attention to activity for, as this will tell you how successful your marketing materials are. Ideally, you should get engagement within the first hour, maximum engagement within the first few hours, and then it should slowly taper off after that over the next day or two. Some pieces of material will continue to float around and produce engagement even after it has lived out its typical life cycle, due to the algorithm seeing it as being a popular material, which is great. When you get content like this, look to see what has made it so successful and see if you can recreate your content in this way.

Monitoring your analytics and adapting your strategy as you go is an excellent way to listen to what your audience wants and give them more of that. This way, rather than launching your products in the way that you *think* people are interested in seeing, you are launching your products in a way that is actually proving to be helpful and useful.

As you do go along with your launch strategy, make sure that you not only adapt your strategy to your analytics but that you also document any adaptations that you have made, and why. This will prove to be helpful in future launches when you are creating your new launch strategies, which is important, as ideally, you want your launch strategy to improve and evolve over time.

In addition to paying attention to analytics and following your schedule, make sure that you spend plenty of time engaging back with other people on your chosen social media platforms, too. Comment back when people comment on your content, and go engage on other people's platforms. Engaging on the platforms of your competitors and your ideal audience will help boost your page up in the algorithm to improve your views, while also putting your name directly in front of more people. When you do engage, seek to go beyond basic "likes" on the post, instead comment, and offer verbal feedback to people when you engage with them. Offer genuine, thoughtful comments that are custom for each post you comment on, rather than generic comments that are known to be seen as spam on most social media platforms. This way, your brand is seen as genuine and authentic and you are more likely to get views from people who you have been engaging with.

Following Your Launch

After you have completed your launch strategy and your product is officially on the market and for sale, there are some follow-up strategies that you need to take into account in order to maximize the success of this launch and any other launch that you do.

The first follow up strategies that you are going to partake indirectly support the launch that you have most recently completed. For this, rather than just letting all of your hard-earned momentum crash as soon as the product has launched, you can use it to keep your product performing for even longer. A great way to carry on with the momentum is to engage with people who have actually purchased your product by thanking them for purchasing from you and sharing their experience with your audience. You can share reviews, user-generated content and more organic posts about these new products and why people love them so much, so that people see that they were worth the investment.

When you are introducing a new product, taking the time to keep the momentum growing after the launch has been completed shows people that the product is as popular as you said it would be. It is common for many people to wait until a product has introduced to see how other people's experiences have gone before they themselves purchase a product, as this is a way to see whether the product was actually worth the investment. As you continue to share the user-generated content that proves that the launch was successful and that people love their products, these people who were awaiting social proof will begin to purchase your products, too. This will keep the momentum of your sales going as more and more people continue to purchase your products.

As the date of your launch passes further away, you are going to want to start reducing the number of posts that you make regarding your most recent launch. At this point, you will resume your standard marketing practices as a way to continue marketing your newer products and all of the other products that you have already had for some time.

Once you reach about one to two weeks after your launch, you want to start doing some post-launch research. This research is your opportunity to identify what was successful about your launch, what helped you get more attention on your products, and what was the least successful part of your launch or what possibly turned attention away. This period is a time for you to honestly assess every single aspect of your launch so that you can take notes and make an even stronger launch plan for the future.

As you research your product launch, this is a great time to overlook the notes that you took during the launch regarding adaptations you made and why they were made. You can use these notes to help you identify what possibly supported you with strengthening your launch and what may have been weakening it along the way. With this, you are going to start evolving your launch blueprint so each time you do a launch going forward you are implementing these new pieces of information that you have learned from previous launches. Over time, you will find that you come up with your own seamless and successful launch strategy that helps you launch successfully every single time. Even so, you should continue to conduct research after every single release, even the highly successful ones that may seem as though they do not need any tweaking or adapting.

In addition to noting down what worked and what did not, do your best to also note down specific analytics that is linked to your launch. In fact, you can even start doing this during the launch in order to get real-time figures regarding the amount of engagement that you were receiving per post, and how that converted into sales once launch day arrived. Keeping track of your analytics is both powerful to help you create strong launch strategies for the future, and a great way to track your growth over time. You should notice that each launch you conduct brings more and more attention to your way, helping you to improve your analytics and increase your engagement. If you find that your analytics are going down or suggesting that your launches are not growing steadily each time, you will need to do some troubleshooting to identify what is interrupting you from growing more successful with each new launch.

Amazon-Specific Tools for Your Launch

In addition to the aforementioned launch strategies that will fit for any e-commerce business in any industry, there are some Amazon-specific tools that you can take advantage of when you are launching new products on Amazon FBA. These tools include things like reviews and Amazon coupons.

In the past, Amazon allowed sellers to incentivize their reviews to encourage people who had purchased from their store to give them a review. This was intended to improve their review ratios so that they had greater credibility backing up their products, thus improving their odds of getting future sales with that particular product. These days, Amazon no longer allows incentives to take place to encourage reviews, which can make collecting reviews a little more challenging. That being said, the review feature is still built into the platform and with a little effort, you can still get great reviews from the individuals who have been purchasing products from your store.

These days, creating reviews takes more follow up on the end of the seller to actually receive the review. Although Amazon will send through a "Thank You" email that offers the customer the opportunity to leave a review, you are going to need to follow up yourself to actually ask for the review. The easiest way to do this is through launching a big blast email to everyone who has purchased from you 4-5 days following them having the product actually delivered into their possession. These follow up emails are easy to create and send out to a large number of people, and they are more likely to earn you reviews over anything else.

The one difficulty with these follow up emails is that you cannot tell which customers have purchased from you and which have not. Rather than playing a guessing game, or sending an irrelevant email to someone who never actually purchased from you, you can instead send out a more generic follow up email that says something like "Hey, if you have already purchased from us, would you care to leave a review? Do so here!" These emails may feel a little more challenging to create, but they actually serve in two great ways. First, they will help people who have purchased from you know where to leave a review, so that they can rave about their new products. Second, if a person did not purchase from you, it reminds them what new product you have available and encourages them to go grab it for themselves. In a way, these emails are more efficient and work as an excellent sales tool, making them worthwhile in the end.

It is important that you create and send out these emails around once per week, or possibly twice per week. You do not need to send them out too often, as this becomes overwhelming and might result in people no longer paying attention to your store. However, remaining consistent with them ensures that they continue to reach people's inboxes and encourage reviews or new sales, both of which are great for helping you grow your business with Amazon FBA.

The other built-in feature that Amazon offers is coupons. Amazon coupons are codes that you can give people that are great for incentivizing sales. Now, understand that based on Amazon is selling policies you are not allowed to exchange discounted sales for reviews, as this can result in your account being banned. When it comes to your business, it is never ideal for you to take risks that could lead to you having something tragic happen, such as having your shop banned, as this can destroy your income. At the end of the day, it is just not worth it.

That being said, you can use coupons to encourage greater sales, which is an excellent opportunity for you to make more sales with your new products. Many sellers use a very specific strategy that helps them offer coupons and encourages greater sales, while also setting them up for future sales, without ever cutting into their bottom line. To do this, they mark up their product an extra 10-15% and then offer a 10-15% off coupon that is exclusive to their social media followers. This encourages people to follow them on social media for special discounts and encourages sales, as people are excited to save 10-15% off their new products. Then, usually, about 2-3 months after the product has launched, the merchant will put the product's official price down 10-15% and market it as having a new lower everyday price. This way, they gain many sales at their ideal price point right from day one, and then they create a new incentive to earn even more sales on that new product a few months later. This is an excellent way to revive momentum around a popular product and earn even more money with your business, without even having to launch a new product to establish more momentum once again.

In addition to offering coupons for first-time buyers, you can also offer coupon codes as a thank you for people who have purchased from you. Offering coupon codes, this way encourages people to purchase from you again in the future, which can secure you more future sales, as well.

When it comes to creating coupons with Amazon, make sure that you are always strategic and logical about it. While coupons can be a wonderful way to increase the number of sales that you gain, it can also cut into your bottom line, if you are not careful. Always calculate what a coupon would truly cost you if every single person were to use one, and never offer more of a discount than you can reasonably manage in your store.

It is also important that you note that any coupon code that exceeds 49% results in the purchasing individual not being able to leave a review that comes from a verified buyer. Although they can still leave a review, Amazon will not give them the "verified purchaser" stamp, which may reduce the credibility of the reviewer for some people. These types of reviews are not given verified buyer stamps because Amazon recognized that many people were simply offering 50%+ off of products in exchange for reviews, so this was a rule put in place to attempt to reduce that behavior.

Chapter 8: Paid Traffic

When considering building your business with Amazon, paid traffic is an incredibly valuable form of traffic that you can earn using AMS, or Amazon Marketing Services. Especially if you want a passive income online, AMS works in the background to continue bringing new customers into your business, without you ever having to do anything beyond the design and pay for an advertisement. This way, you can continue earning new sales, even without creating more organic content for your audience to reach.

If you want to run a successful Amazon FBA business, you should be prepared to rely on both paid and organic traffic in order to really drive your sales up. Paid traffic is often going to be the easiest and most targeted traffic; however, organic traffic is built in a way that establishes credibility and recognition for your brand making it valuable as well.

Many merchants rely exclusively on AMS to bring sales into their businesses and never actually bother with setting up a brand, or creating any form of online presence beyond their actual Amazon storefront. Of course, this is not recommended because it does you a disservice by not using simple tools to build your credibility, establish momentum, and grow your business as rapidly as possible. However, it is a method that you could use if you wanted your Amazon FBA business to be as hands-off as possible and you had the budget to exclusively market in this way.

Creating a combined approach with both organic and paid marketing is ideal, so for best results, you should use AMS in addition to organic marketing to create your strongest impact. So far, we have discussed a lot regarding organic marketing strategies that you can use to get your business in front of your target audience. Now, we are going to discuss how you can use Amazon AMS ads to improve your visibility, increase your sales, and even further maximize your momentum for the purpose of growing the largest business possible.

Amazon AMS Ads

Amazon's Canadian platform attracts more than 15 million unique visitors every single month, and more than 20.6 million unique visitors land on Amazon's American platform every single month. As well, more than 80% of the people who visit Amazon report that they are ready to purchase products right away or in the near future, so they are landing on the platform because they are ready to purchase something new?

When you choose to use Amazon's AMS service with your Amazon FBA store, you give yourself the opportunity to get your products directly in front of the targeted portion of this population. This means that Amazon will identify users who are most likely to purchase what you are promoting and they will show it to them, earning you an increased number of traffic to your own posts. The greatest part of Amazon AMS is that you do not have to attempt to figure out an algorithm and fight against several other merchants for the best placement on the page, in order to be viewed by possible customers. Instead, because you have paid for space, you are shown right away and you earn guaranteed viewers in whatever volume your budget has accounted for.

On average, the merchants who use sponsored advertisements in the United States to see about a 7x return on their ad spend, meaning that they earn massive profits from the amount of money that they invest into their advertisements. With this average, one $100 advertisement could earn you $700 or more in revenue for your storefront, which is a massive profit in the end. For this reason, it is obvious as to why Amazon AMS is such a powerful tool for you to be using, when you are growing your Amazon FBA business.

When it comes to creating an advertisement with AMS, there are three products that you can use to get your advertisements in front of your audience. These include sponsored products, sponsored brands, and product display ads. Sponsored products are products that merchants pay to have featured at the top of a search ranking, so that they land first on the results page over any other merchant or product that the search brings up. Sponsored brand advertisements are advertisements that feature your brand logo in prominent areas on Amazon's website to help increase your brand awareness and drive more traffic to your store. Product display ads (PDA) allow products to be displayed in various places across Amazon's website, so that as people are scrolling and shopping they are also seeing your products show up around the page. All three of these advertisement styles are excellent for driving more traffic to your store or product pages, making it much easier for you to earn sales through Amazon FBA.

In the matter of creating your Amazon FBA store, it is important that you set aside a reasonable budget for you to create AMS advertisements with. At least $100 should be set aside, however, $200-$500 would be even better to help you launch your store with, in order to receive more traffic to your storefront. Ideally, you should set a budget that is proportionate to the amount of product that you will be receiving, so that you have plenty of product to serve the amount of traffic that you will be sent to your store through these advertisements. That way, you do not spend too much on advertising and find yourself running out of product before your full ad budget is even spent, or having a large amount of product left even though your ad budget has already run out.

Getting Started With an AMS Ads Account

Before you can begin creating advertisements with Amazon, you are going to need to create an Amazon Advertising Console account. Advertisements are not able to be done through your standard Amazon Seller Central account, so make sure to go create this new ad account, first. You can create your Amazon Advertising Console account by simply going to the website, which can be found on Google, and following the directions on screen to launch your account. Note that Amazon's Advertising Console used to be called Amazon Marketing Services, but the account itself is now called Advertising Console. The services you are using are still AMS, but their branding has shifted in the recent past.

When you create your account, you are going to need to include your personal information, as well as some information about the store that you run on Amazon. This way, you can link your store to your Amazon Advertisement Console account and create advertisements with Amazon that are specifically for your existing products.

Designing and Promoting Your AMS Ads

Once your advertisement account is made, you can begin to create and promote advertisements on your AMS account. Creating your advertisements with AMS is incredibly simple, as the platform has set it out in a systematic process, making it easy for you to choose which type of advertisement you want to create and whom you want to advertise it to. Below, we are going to discuss the exact process that you will follow for creating advertisements for your Amazon FBA store, so that you can design strong advertisements that are going to earn you the most sales on Amazon.

The first step is to log into your Advertisement Console and identify what type of advertisement you want to promote. For maximum results, you will want to promote multiple advertisements, as this will have plenty of different advertisements out there drawing attention back to your shop and encouraging people to buy from you. Ideally, you should have at least one of each kind of advertisement active at all times. For now, start with just one and follow the steps all the way through, then follow the exact same steps for every future advertisement that you choose to promote as well. This way, every single advertisement is made with the same high-quality standards that will earn you the best results with that advertisement.

Once you have chosen what type of advertisement you want to create for your store, you will follow the systematic process on screen to build your advertisements. For Sponsored Product ads, this is as simple as choosing the product that you want to promote and then promoting that product with your chosen target audience and budget. These advertisements are published right away and do not require any review. For Sponsored Brands and Product Display Ads, you will need to design what is called "ad creative", which features imagery and text that helps promote either your brand or your product. In either case, you are going to need to have your advertisement approved by moderation, which can take up to 72 hours on the Amazon platform.

When you are using Sponsored Brands or Product Display Advertisements on Amazon, you want to make sure that you are using the highest quality graphics possible for your images. Your logo should be high quality and appropriate, and any products you might be displaying should be high quality and easy to see and identify in a display advertisement. The better the quality of graphics that you use on your advertisements, the better your chances of getting people to actually click on to your advertisements, because they are more interesting and attractive to your ideal target audience.

Once your advertisements are up and running, the only thing that you need to do is track the analytics that is related to your advertisements. You want to pay attention to make sure that they are working and that they are bringing in business to your products, to ensure that you are actually earning a return on your advertisements. If you find that something needs to be adjusted in order to improve their results, you should make those adjustments right away. It is important that you do not check-in and adjust your advertisements more than once per week, as this can result in you making too many changes to receive accurate results from your advertisements. Checking once per week gives you plenty of time to accumulate data and identify reasonable adjustments, without letting too long go in between checks, which could result in costly mistakes on your end, if you are not careful.

When you do run advertisements for your shop, it is ideal to run a never-ending advertisement that you have to manually turn off, rather than to run one that is going to end after a certain period. Attempting to redesign and reapprove advertisements every few days or weeks can get time-consuming, especially if you are advertising the same products anyway. Furthermore, you lose all of the live data surrounding that particular advertisement, which can result in you not having access to all of the information that you need to make a new advertisement just as successful. Creating a never-ending advertisement will ensure that you never miss a sales opportunity and that your advertisements keep working for you.

With Amazon's AMS, there are three types of payment strategies that you can take advantage of to help you pay for the advertisements that you are making with your business. These payments include pay per click, pay per day, and pay per campaign. Each payment strategy works slightly differently and will result in your budget being used in a different way. You can choose either strategy that you prefer, as each one has its benefits and drawbacks for how it will affect your ability to run your ads.

Pay per click is the most flexible, lenient option that is going to help you get the most out of your advertisement. When you do pay per click advertisements, there is no cap on how frequently your advertisement is shown to anyone and you only pay when someone actually clicks on it. In this case, if 100 people per day are clicking it, then you pay for 100 people per day. The advertisement will not be capped at any point due to your budget running out, which could result in you missing sales. The nice thing about pay per click, too, is that you bid on how much you want to pay per ad click and you can feel confident that you will never pay more than that amount on your clicks. This means that you can still reasonably track and control your expenses, without putting a limit on how many clicks you can receive per day.

Pay per day means that you set a daily budget and your budget will not exceed that amount per day. Amazon will continue to show your advertisement to people until that budget is reached, and then the advertisement will not be shown again until the next day when your budget refreshes. While this can make budgeting more predictable, it can also result in you missing many potential sales, if you are using up your budget rather early on. Since sales are what give you the best return on your marketing budget, this is not exactly ideal. Still, this might be a good option early on to help you stick to a consistent budget, and start to accumulate data about how much it costs per click so that you know how much to bid on a click in future advertisements.

Pay per campaign is the most predictable, which makes it an excellent method of marketing for budgets. When you use pay per campaign, you are able to easily write off your budget and feel confident that you are spending an exact amount. As well, your advertisements will not be capped until you reach your budget, which means that there will be no limit on how many people see your advertisement per day until you reach that amount. That being said, depending on what you are paying per click you may end up spending your entire budget rather quickly, leaving you with nothing left toward the end of your campaign. Furthermore, pay per campaign option is only available to Sponsored Brands and Product Display Ads, and it is not available to Sponsored Product ads.

Overall, it can be helpful to use either pay per campaign or pay per day budgeting methods, until you begin to accumulate data with your advertisements that give you an idea as to how much the average click costs in your industry. Then, once you begin to have a clearer idea of what that number is, you can start bidding that amount on pay per click advertisements and letting your advertisements run indefinitely. Although this may sound scary as you could potentially have a large advertising bill, it also gives you the best odds of reaching your 7x return on your ad budget, which is ideal when you want to run an Amazon FBA store and earn passive income.

Advertisement Advice from Existing Merchants

To help you get a head start with AMS so that you can earn even more through your advertisements, I have compiled a list of some of the best tips for how you can maximize your advertising budget and earn a high income through your Amazon ads. Using this guide will help you really put your ads to work, improving your passive income potential and earning you as much as possible through your Amazon FBA business. Be sure to consider these tips when creating your own advertisements in the Advertisement Console, with the purpose of creating successful advertisements that actually earn you a high return.

The first thing you need to do when it comes to creating advertisements is gathered with strong keywords for your business. Some merchants recommend gathering at least 300 high-quality keywords, so that you can write ad content that features several high-quality keywords to help promote your ad. The more relevant keywords that your ad has, the more likely you are going to show up for people in your target audience, so do not overlook this part.

You should also use manual targeting, even though Amazon has a built-in targeting feature that often has people thinking that it is the most useful selection. Having said that, manual targeting can sometimes be off and can leave you struggling to actually reach the people who are most likely to purchase your products. Through manual targeting, you can do your own research, plug in your own metrics, and slowly adapt them as you go, so that you can hit the perfect target audience that is going to be the most likely to purchase your products on Amazon.

When you first start out with advertising on Amazon, it is ideal to allow a small budget to several smaller campaigns, so that when you begin advertising everything is modest. This is a great way for you to get your name and products out there, while also accumulating strong data that will tell you exactly what types of advertisements work and which do not, and what demographics and metrics best suit your advertisements. Once you begin to understand the data, you can start, increasing your budget and minimizing the number of campaigns that you are running at any given time, so that you can start earning higher results on your campaigns.

As soon as you start to find campaign setups that are proving to be effective, increase your budget with that particular campaign. Start with something simple like $10 a day and then grow from there, as this is a great opportunity for you to increase your budget and your income at a modest yet consistent rate. This is also a great opportunity for you to invest in a tested and proven advertisement, rather than throwing a huge budget into an advertisement that has not yet been tested on your platform.

When it comes to advertisements, you need to be patient. Especially before you have an established reputation, you are going to need time for people to see these advertisements and actually take action on them. Some studies have suggested that it takes 346 total store visits before someone actually purchases from you, while others say it could take 2-3 weeks. Just because you do not start making immediate returns on your investment does not mean that your advertisement is not working, it just means that it is taking its time, like most standard advertisements do. Be patient and it will pick up, and then the momentum will continue growing over time.

For the advertisements that are absolutely not performing, as in they are not receiving any impressions or they are not receiving enough impressions to be worthwhile, you need to scrap the entire advertisement altogether. It is better to start from scratch than it is to repeatedly tweak an advertisement that has proven to be ineffective.

Finally, if you are getting a high number of impressions but you are not receiving many clicks with your advertisement, it is because you are not creating advertisements that are interesting to your audience. You need to create a new campaign that is interesting and that actually attracts attention from your audience and try again in this case, in order to earn a greater conversion ratio with your advertisements.

By following this advice to help maximize your conversions and success with Amazon advertisements, you should be able to create high-quality advertisements that product excellent conversion ratio for your business. Over time, you will start to understand exactly what it takes to create high performing ads on Amazon and it will be much easier, as you will not have to fuss quite so much with different campaigns and ad styles to finally find the one that works best for you. This skill improves as you understand Amazon better, as well as you start to understand you are own demographic better, making it easier for you to understand in advance what they are looking for and what is most likely to capture their attention for a sale.

Chapter 9: The Most Important Things to Grow Your Amazon Business

Growing your Amazon business requires you to not only start it and create a successful first launch, but also to maintain it and continue growing it every single day. As you already know, you are going to be required to launch multiple products and continue to build buzz around your business, if you are going to generate any level of success. The more that you can increase awareness around your business and grow your business out, the more sales you are going to make and, in turn, the more profits you will make as well. This way, you can create maximum sales through your business, which will allow you to earn even more over time.

Many people think that growing your business means that you will have to put in even more work to keep your business running, but the truth is that you can grow your business and still keep it highly passive, if you want to. The key is to automate wherever you can, so that you can leverage more platforms and strategies without having to use up too much more of your time. In addition to automation, you want to stay consistent in your strategies and stick to what you know. This way, running your business stays easy and you continue to produce the same great results that you have already been producing all along.

In this chapter, we are going to discuss how you can grow your business without massively increasing your workload. This way, you can improve your profits, increase your revenue, and create an even stronger income through Amazon FBA without taking up too much more of your time.

Stay Consistent, Use What Works

When it comes to growing your Amazon FBA business, you want to use what works and remain consistent in how you approach your business. Consistency provides benefits to your business in many different ways, including in ways that directly influence both you and your customer. The impacts that consistency has on both parties is important, as it makes running your business easier, and it makes relying on your business and trusting in your quality of products and services easier.

Regarding yourself and your business, remaining consistent makes running your business easier because you already know what you are doing. As you repeat the same launch processes and growth strategies repeatedly, you will find that despite some of the details changing, the consistency in the strategy makes generating success a breeze. With consistency in this area, you prevent yourself from having to completely design new strategies from scratch every single time you want to launch a new product or market in a new way. This way, rather than starting from scratch, you can improve on the practices that you have already been using and continue to refine and evolve your tried and true practices over time. In the end, this is going to make running your business much easier and will contribute to your success in both maintaining and growing your business over the years.

With your audience, consistency gives them something to rely on and trust in. When your audience sees you using the same launch strategies repeatedly, they are more likely to trust in what you have to offer because they come to know your strategies, too. As they see, your strategies put into action repeatedly, it cultivates a consistent image in their minds of who you are and what you have to offer. This leaves no room for confusion or overwhelm, and ensures that there is no reason for your customers to think that you do not have a clear sense of direction with what you are doing. Instead, they see you using your consistent approach and they recognize it as being your style and personality thrown into your brand, effectively marketing your business. In other words, your consistency becomes a part of your image and actually improves your brand loyalty.

Companies that are known to change their approaches too frequently often destroy their momentum and lose their audience's attention and loyalty because no one can keep up with what they are doing. Their customers grow confused with the way things work, are unaware of what is going on with the business at any given time, and do not feel confident in the company or the way that they do business. The company's inability to commit to any given strategy often comes across as being flaky or unreliable, which can massively reduce the quality of their reputation. In the end, it pays to be predictable and repetitive in your approach, and keep your customers developing curiosity through the details.

Extend Your Online Presence

Social media is a powerhouse when it comes to marketing, no matter what you are marketing for. If you want to grow your brand awareness and increase your traffic to your website, using social media is a great opportunity for you to do so. In fact, when you have to grow your business on Amazon FBA and get more traffic into your store, social media is actually a key player.

Extending your online presence essentially means that you put more effort into being active and engaged on multiple platforms, while also leveraging the strategies available on those platforms to help you grow. For example, if you are presently using Instagram and Facebook to market your products, you could extend your online presence by using Twitter, YouTube, and even Pinterest or LinkedIn to begin marketing your products to your target audience. When you do extend your online presence, make sure that you are extending into platforms where your audience actually spends time, so that you are more likely to get right in front of them. This way, you are making the extension of your presence worthwhile, which will ultimately help you grow your business rapidly with social media.

As you do extend your presence, you want to take advantage of the services that each platform has to offer when it comes to marketing. You can also take advantage of marketing automation to ensure that your platforms stay active and engaged, even when you are not presently using them. This is a great way to keep your platforms passive while still earning you a greater presence and income.

Concerning leveraging marketing tools on social media, one of the biggest features you should focus on is native advertising. Native advertisements are paid promotions that exist directly on any given social media platform, and that often fall in line with their newsfeed so that they see it amongst their existing posts.

When it comes to growing your presence, these native advertisements can offer you the same benefits that AMS advertisements offer you, further extending your reach without much effort on your behalf. Including native advertisements on social media platforms as a part of your ad budget, is a great opportunity to reach even more people and drive even more traffic to your Amazon store, further improving your sales reach.

Automate Wherever You Can
When it comes to growing your business while still maintaining the passive element of it, it pays to automate whenever and wherever you can. Automation is a powerful tool that can help you stay active on social media, or any other platform, without actually having to physically log on and partake in activities on that platform on a regular basis. Running your business through automation earns you time freedom while your business still stays active enough to earn you an income, which earns you financial freedom, too.

For advertisements, the automation ultimately comes from paying them to exist, and then only needing to check in on them once per week to make sure that they are still performing properly and earning you a strong income. These are one of the best ways to run automation, as they guarantee you some form of attention to your advertisements and help you grow your business rapidly and successfully.

Another automation feature that you can use is accomplished by using a platform like *HootSuite* or *HubSpot*. These platforms allow you to log in to all of your social media accounts on one single platform, then create, and schedule posts for those platforms ahead of time. For many of them, you can create a single post and have it sent out to multiple different social media platforms in a single go, maximizing the use of that particular post and making it easier for you to be found online. When you do get started using automation platforms, make sure that you automate no further than one to two weeks in advance, as automating too far in advance can leave you with outdated marketing materials, should you find that trends change and your materials are all geared toward outdated trends. Moreover, checking in weekly or bi-weekly helps you monitor analytics and ensure that your posts are getting excellent results, improving your chances at growing your presence on these platforms more consistently and rapidly.

The Value of Momentum

Momentum, as you know, is a valuable tool to have in place when we talk about launching new products and earning sales with new product lines. That being said, momentum is not exclusive to new product launches when it comes to growing your business. If you want to grow your Amazon FBA business consistently, you want to make sure that you are leveraging momentum in every way possible with your business. The best way to do this is to make sure that you are paying attention to every opportunity that you are receiving with your business, and to take advantage of as many of them as you possibly can. The more opportunities that you take advantage of, the more times you are going to get your business seen by a new audience and the more sales that you are going to make overall. This is crucial if you want to be successful with Amazon FBA, so it is important that you be always on the lookout or in the process of making new opportunities for yourself to take.

When you do take up these new opportunities, do not rely on them exclusively to build your momentum. Instead, leverage them in every way possible so that you can maximize the amount of momentum that you are gaining from each opportunity. This way, not only you are getting direct benefits from the opportunities themselves, but you are also getting benefits from talking about these opportunities and building your audience's excitement in them, too. The more that you can combine new opportunities by talking about new opportunities, the more momentum you are going to continue to grow in your business, which will lead to increased success.

You can track your momentum by paying attention to your analytics. If at any point you find your business is not growing the way you desire it to, chances are you can find the exact problem directly in your analytics. Below, we will discuss the value of your analytics and how you can use them to guide your business forward.

Use Your Analytics to Guide You

As I have mentioned throughout this book, your analytics are a powerful source of data that can directly tell you what your audience may not be willing to say aloud. When you use your analytics to guide you, you can feel confident that you are directly listening to what your audience wants more of an offer more of what they are looking for. This way, as you continue to share new pieces of marketing materials with your audience, you can feel confident that every single piece is going to succeed with reaching your audience and generating success for your business.

In the matter of reading your analytics, there is a simple system for reading them to ensure that your posts are gaining traction. First, you want to see how many people saw the post, and then you want to see how many people engaged with the post. Ideally, you want to have at least a 2-8% or higher engagement ratio, as this tends to be a standard ratio on most platforms. You might have some pieces of content that perform at 30% + engagement ratios and others that perform lower than 2%. Naturally, you want to look at each piece of content and start seeing what the differences are, in order to begin to understand why some contents perform well, and why other contents do not.

If you look at the content that thrives versus the content that struggles, you should be able to identify some obvious differences or patterns that highlight why some products work and why others do not. You might notice nuances as if your underperforming content has lower quality graphics or graphics that all feature similar content that, for some reason or another, does not seem to resonate well with your audience. Or, you might find that there are certain topics that you are talking about in either that is causing your audience to like or ignore the content that you have created. As you notice these patterns, jot them down and keep track of them, as this is going to help you understand your audience better.

Ideally, you should be reading your analytics every single week, especially right before you begin to create new content for your platforms. Reading your analytics before creating new content can help you create new content that is actually relevant to what your audience wants to see and read about. This way, you are more likely to create new content that performs even better than previous content.

The more that you create higher quality, relevant content for your audience, the more you are going to recognize your positive momentum growing in your favor and helping you expand your business reach. This will help your analytic tracking work together with leveraging your momentum to help you grow your business and earn more sales over time.

Build Out Your Product Line

The final and perhaps most obvious way for you to grow your Amazon FBA business is to continually add new products to your product line. After your initial launch with all of your new products in your new store, you want to start adding new products to your shop on a consistent basis. The key to building out your product line is that you want to be consistent, but not overwhelming. This way, you are going to have plenty to talk about and grow into, without bombarding your audience with constant back-to-back launches, which can be overwhelming and can actually drive your audience away. Although they do want to see that you are growing and adding new options or products for them to order, they do not want to constantly hear from you with your new offerings, as this may desensitize them and cause them to ignore your new launches.

Most successful companies choose to launch a new lineup of products every 3 months or every quarter. This gives them an entire quarter to devote to choosing these new products, organizing the launch, and conducting the launch, then conducting the launch follow up and then to grow momentum in between with standard marketing practices. If you choose to do this, you can perfect a 3-month marketing strategy complete with all of the aforementioned marketing cycles for every new product lineup that you add to your business. This way, you always know what you are marketing for and you have an easy time-sharing your new products with your audience.

If you do choose to build out your product line with lineups like this every three months, it is important that you slightly alter your product research phase to look for products that are likely going to be popular for the next season. After all, you do not want to be marketing for last season's products in the new season when you do each new marketing launch. For example, you do not want to be marketing cozy sweaters or Christmas gift items in the spring when you start your new launch cycles. Make sure that you are always being realistic about what is popular now and what is likely to remain popular come your launch cycle, so that you are stocking up on products that are more likely to sell.

The alternative to doing quarterly launches is to launch a new product every month or every other month. This way, your launch cycle would look more like spending 1-2 weeks in the launch phase, launching a new product, and spending 1-2 weeks in follow up phase as you build on the momentum of that new product. By the time, that product has been out for a couple of weeks, you can start preparing for the launch of your next product. This style of marketing is like taking baby steps with your momentum by growing it out consistently over time, without ever really taking a beat between your marketing strategies.

If you do choose to market this way, make sure that you take periodic breaks in between your launches to give your audience a chance to take a break, too. Remember: your audience is not going to want to buy something new from you every single month as they have other things they want to purchase, too. Unless you have a massive audience that cycles between who buys each month, you are going to generate your best success this way by launching a new product every 6-8 weeks, so that there is plenty of time between each launch for your audience to recover and prepare for a new launch.

Chapter 10: The Right Mindset to Sell

When it comes to building a business, marketing, and growing your success, your mindset plays a huge role in the success that you can generate for yourself. In the past, it was somewhat of a secret that your mindset mattered in the level of success that you could create for yourself, but these days it seems to be knowledge that is more common. People are starting to realize that if they do not genuinely believe in themselves and what they are doing, they are not going to be likely to generate any success with their businesses. Believing in yourself is only part of it though: you also need to have the right attitude and approach toward the various elements of business and marketing to ensure that you are ready to generate a strong success for yourself in e-commerce.

In this chapter, I am going to show you some of the best advice from top sellers in various e-commerce platforms, in order to prepare yourself and your mindset for success. I strongly advise you to take this in and begin to leverage this mindset in your own life so that you are personally, emotionally, and mentally prepared to face any of the challenges or circumstances that may arise when you are running your Amazon FBA business.

Surround Yourself with the Right Influence

The first thing that you need to pay attention to when it comes to developing the right mindset for you to create success in your business is the influence that you have surrounded yourself with. Each of us has surrounded ourselves with various people and circumstances that influence the way we feel, the way we perceive things, and the way we behave in various scenarios. If your current influences are not supporting you with feeling confident, empowered, and eager to create success in your Amazon business, it can massively inhibit your ability to proceed through many of the growth challenges that you will face. The biggest reason for this is that you may find yourself feeling discouraged, as if you are attempting to face the impossible, or even embarrassed by the challenges that you are facing, due to the people that you have surrounded yourself by. The truth is, everyone faces these growth challenges and finds themselves struggling from time to time, even in a business model as simple as Amazon FBA. If the wrong people surround you, these challenges can seem catastrophic and as though they are impossible for you to grow past.

If you surround yourself with the right people, however, you are going to find yourself seeing these challenges as being natural, normal, and passable. Rather than laying down in defeat, you will be more likely to begin searching for answers for ways that you can get beyond these challenges, so that you can continue growing with your business. This way, you are far more likely to actually pass the challenges because you are *trying.*

When it comes to surrounding yourself by the right influences, you need to do it in every way possible. This means that you should seek to befriend and spend time with people who are also building their own businesses. You should also add more empowering and motivational content to your personal life by following pages or groups on social media that are inspiring and helpful, reading inspiring and helpful books, and otherwise surrounding yourself with positive influence. In addition to surrounding yourself with positive influence, you also need to be working toward minimizing the negative influence in your circle. This does not mean that you have to stop being friend with people who do not agree with your business or who do not believe in your ability to succeed, but it does mean that you need to have strong boundaries. In these relationships, firmly refuse to discuss anything relating to your business, to avoid being exposed to negative influence by these individuals. This way, you can feel confident that you can continue to engage in these relationships without them negatively rubbing off on you in your business.

Practice Doing Your Best Every Single Time

Although you are going to be focusing on the "rinse and repeat" efforts in your business by creating a system of strategies that work for you and then executing them again and again, you still want to practice doing your best every single time. No matter how passive you build your income to be, you never want to become complacent in the way that you approach the work, that you do need to exert into running your business. As soon as you begin to become complacent and behave as though it is completely impossible for you to screw it up, you are going to start putting shoddy quality work into your business and your customers will recognize it. This is a surefire way to quickly destroy your business and can lead to you rapidly losing the income that you have worked so hard to generate.

Rather than growing complacent, set out with the mindset to do your very best every single time you do something for your business. Whether it is researching for new products, creating product page descriptions, launching new AMS advertisements, or engaging on your social media profiles, always seek to do your absolute best every single time. The more that you can commit to doing the best that you can, the better each strategy is going to be, as you grow more used to seeing it through. This way, you can continue to refine and perfect your strategies over time and you can feel confident that you are effectively evolving them, and applying them every single time you put them into action.

When you do aim to do your best every single time, it is important that you focus on doing just that: you are *best*. One mistake many people make when it comes to something more serious like running a business is aiming for perfect, which can drive anyone crazy. If you attempt to do everything perfectly right from day one, you are going to struggle in your business because it simply is not possible. Even massive companies who have been at it for generations still struggle with certain things or make mistakes that set them below the bar of being "perfect." If you aim for perfection, you are going to scrutinize and criticize every single element of your business and you will never be satisfied with what you are creating for yourself.

When you do work on a piece of marketing material, do your best. Look it over, make sure that you have applied every piece of knowledge that you have to the best of your ability, and ask yourself if you are proud of it. If you feel that you have done everything, the way you believe you were supposed to have done it and you are proud of it, you have done excellently. You can go ahead and launch that material, and then use any feedback or analytics that you retrieve from that material to help you do even better next time. If there were not room for improvement, you would have nothing to grow into, so be grateful for this growth room and be proud of doing your best.

Leverage Your Surroundings for Success

Regarding building a business, your surroundings can actually have a huge impact on your level of success. Many people find that they have to be in a certain situation or environment, in order for them to feel clear enough to focus on doing the work that needs to be done. For example, if you have worked at an office job all of your life, attempting to work from home might seem nearly impossible because you have always spent your time at home relaxing and enjoying yourself, rather than working.

Creating the right environment for you to work and thrive in is important for you to get in the frame of mind to help you succeed. You can do this by understanding what it takes you to feel ready to work and then by creating that exact environment for you to get started. This could be anything from creating a clean office with a nice desk and a photograph of your family on your desk to help you be focused, to heading out to a local café with your laptop to help you be focused. Consider what environment helps you feel the most focused and productive, and then go to that environment to start your work process. When you are in an environment that gets you in the right frame of mind and keeps you focused, you are more likely to produce consistent and high-quality work, which makes it well worth the effort to put yourself in the right environment to get the job done.

Understand Your Customers' Needs and Wants

A big mistake that new business owners make is being caught up in the details that they read in books just like this one while forgetting about what really matters. If you want to be successful in your business, you need to remember that your customers' needs and wants come before everything else in your business. After all, your customers are the ones who are going to be purchasing from you and if they are not having their needs or wants to be met, they are not going to want to purchase anything from you. Instead, they are going to go to another business that is offering them exactly what they are looking for.

When you begin to run your own Amazon FBA business, make a point to get into and stay in the mindset of understanding what your customers need and want and how you can fulfill those needs and wants. Always put their desires at the top of your businesses focus and do all that you can to make sure that they are being fulfilled. If at any point you notice a common complaint or pattern in feedback rising, consider those and begin to look for ways to adapt to serve your customers' needs in a better way.

At the end of the day, it does not matter if you want to sell a certain product or run your business in a certain way, if your customers prove that this is not what they are seeking. Honor your customers and they will always have a strong reason to come back to your business to buy from you. As a result, you will always have an audience to sell to and a business to grow with.

Focus on How You Can Help Your Customers
In addition to fulfilling your customers' wants and needs, also look for how you can help your customers. This particular mindset is powerful when it comes to sales in particular, rather than just growth itself. Concerning selling things to your product, always look at it from the perspective that you are looking to sell something to them, so that you can help them. In one way or another, you are helping them live a better life with your product and that is exactly why they have come to you and why they want to purchase from you in the first place.

A huge reserve that many people who are new to e-commerce have is around selling, because they are afraid that they are being pushy or ignorant when they sell their products. Of course, this is not true, but if you are not used to marketing and selling things it can be easy to feel as if this is true and you are a nuisance to other people.

If you always focus on searching for ways that you can help people with your products, then you can feel confident that you are always approaching your marketing in a way that is respectful and not pushy. Furthermore, the people who are interested in what you have to offer will gather, while the people who are not interested will stay away. Remember: they are choosing to follow you and engage with your business, you are not forcing it on them. You are just there to helpfully offer products that can fulfill their needs and desires, and help them enjoy life even more. There is nothing wrong with what you are doing, and you can confidently approach your business, marketing, and sales knowing that you are working from a positive and kind-hearted place.

Practice Stepping into the Mode of "Listener"

The final step that is crucial when it comes to building a business is being the "listener." With marketing, your primary goal is to attract people to your business, which means that you need to be "loud" to get your name out there and get people paying attention to what you have to offer. It can be easy to forget that you will not know what to say, if you do not know what people are interested in hearing.

Stepping into the role of the listener with your business allows you to pay attention to what your audience wants, to discover how you can fulfill those wants, and to create a business that directly serves them. You can step into the role of listening by

96

listening to what people say directly to you, paying attention to your analytics and listening to the people in your niche in general. Follow blogs, the competition, and even people who are great prospects for being clients of your business, and listen to what they have to say. Everywhere you are receiving access to information that is crucial to helping you grow your business in the most effective way possible, so make sure to take the time to listen and then respond to the market.

This way, you truly can step into the role of an industry leader and earn the most money that you can possibly earn through your Amazon FBA business.

Chapter 11: FAQ

Before I send you off to start your own Amazon FBA business and officially start running it as a gig for you to earn a consistent income from, I want to answer a few more questions for you. Starting a new business can come with many questions, and I want to make sure that you feel as confident as you possibly can in what you have learned here in this book.

In this chapter, we are going to explore some of the top questions that people have with Amazon FBA and the answers to those questions. This way, as you begin to run your business, you can feel confident that you are doing it properly.

How Do I Compute How Many Products to Send to Amazon FBA?

Concerning shipping products to the Amazon warehouse, you want to make sure that you are sending enough so that you can fulfill your orders, but not so much that you struggle to sell all of your stock. Finding that perfect amount takes some practice, but there are also a few factors that you can consider to help you make a perfect judgment call.

A great program to use for this is "Economic Order Quantity", which allows you to calculate the best number of products to send to Amazon FBA. With this platform, you need to first identify how quickly products are turning around for the company, how much demand there is, and how much the ordering costs are. Then, the program will give you the perfect number of products to order.

Early on, finding the exact numbers can be challenging, as you do not already have your own data on this. However, you can conduct some basic Google research to help you identify these statistics to give you an average estimate to help you get started.

What are the Minimum Amazon FBA Packaging Requirements?

Amazon is relaxed when it comes to packaging requirements, so long as your packaging fully covers the unit and is protective of the products inside. That being said, everything from cardboard sleeves and cardboard boxes to plastic sleeves and even bags are all plenty for you to package your products with. So long as they are clearly labeled for tracking and inventory purposes, you should be perfectly fine.

When it comes to cartons, you need to make sure that they are less than 50lbs and are no longer, wider, or taller than 24 inches. You can also not have more than 500 products in a single carton, as this exceeds Amazon's maximum quantity in a carton.

How Do I Use Amazon FBA with Third-Party Stores?

Amazon FBA offers what is known as "multi-channel fulfillment", which means that you can list, market, and sell your products with third-party stores and still have Amazon fulfill their part of the packaging, shipping, and managing your inventory. That being said, there is a learning curve to using third-party stores to sell your products on Amazon so that you can use this multi-channel fulfillment service properly. Something worth noting is that even though your customer may have purchased through a platform like Shopify, Etsy, or even your own website, it will still ship in an Amazon-branded box. This typically does not affect most people's decision to stock their stores this way, but it is something to consider when it comes to branding.

To use multi-channel fulfillment services, you first want to set up the alternative channel where your products will be offered for sale. Once they are all set up, make sure that they do not yet go live. You do not want people ordering stock until the Amazon FBA part is set up, otherwise, you will run into issues with the order being processed and fulfilled by Amazon FBA employees.

Next, you need to go to your Amazon account and tap "Fulfillment by Amazon." Then, tap "Edit Multi-Channel Fulfillment Settings" There, you want to turn on the multi-channel fulfillment features which enable you to submit manual requests for orders to be processed elsewhere.

When it comes to processing orders through Amazon FBA with third-party fulfillment services, you will always have to submit a manual request for the service to be fulfilled. You can do so by going to Seller Central, uploading an XML template, and then choosing your delivery options. Lastly, you want to confirm the order and then Amazon will process it by picking, packing, and shipping this order.

Unlike with Amazon FBA storefronts, you will be responsible for offering customer service and managing any returns or exchanges, so you should be prepared to take care of any of these concerns should the need arise.

With all this being said, many people believe that using Amazon FBA to fulfill multi-channel sales is not worthwhile because it costs too much and requires too much effort on behalf of the seller. If you want to be a passive business owner, this is not the way to build a passive, sustainable business with unlimited growth for your business. Therefore, if you do decide to do this, you should consider it carefully and make sure that you really are making the right decision for your end goal.

How Do I Ship my Products to FBA Warehouses?

Getting your products shipped to Amazon may seem daunting, but it is actually incredibly simple. To do so, you will need to log into your Amazon Seller Central account and go to the "Manage Inventory" option. If you are shipping brand new items to Amazon FBA, you will need to add a new inventory item to your inventory stock list. Otherwise, select the items on your inventory list that you want to ship to the warehouse and tap "Action on Selected", then click "Send/Replenish Inventory." With that done, you can create a shipping plan as per the instructions in Chapter 5.

After you have completed all of the steps to process the shipment, you will be given an address for where you can ship your products. Amazon has countless warehouses, so it is important that you use this address and not any other address, as you want to make sure that they go to the right warehouse. With that done, you can process your order and Amazon will be ready to receive it.

Amazon Labeled my Products as an "Add On" Item, What Can I Do?

Since the release of Amazon Prime, Amazon has begun to label certain items for sale as "Add On" items, which means that customers have to purchase something else in order to purchase your item. If you did not intend for this to happen, it can be frustrating as this can drastically limit your sales by requiring people to purchase more than they want to purchase. Although this is intended to be an up-sell feature for Amazon, which can increase sales, it can also put a serious damper on sales for individual merchants.

If this happens to one of your products, the likely cause is that the product is too inexpensive, which means that it is not worth Amazon shipping costs to send the product individually. In this case, you can either leave the product as an add on and factor this into your consideration, when it comes to restocking the product, or you can raise the cost of the product. Raising the cost of the product can improve the cash value, which might help Amazon determine that it is worth the shipping costs on, which will turn it back into an independent item. There is rarely an alternative solution to this situation, so you will want to consider this whenever it comes to stocking products that are particularly inexpensive, such as those that are under $10 and especially on those that are under $5.

How Do I Sell Overseas with Amazon FBA?

When it comes to selling on Amazon FBA, one of the best benefits of it is that you immediately tap into a global market and the opportunity to sell to people anywhere in the world. This includes selling to people who are overseas, or who are not present in the North American marketplace. Amazon does, however, host different websites for each of their marketplaces, so you are going to have to adjust some settings on your Amazon Seller Central account to be able to sell to these corresponding marketplaces.

To sell overseas, you will need to start by creating inventory lists in the right marketplace for where you want to sell. For example, if you want to sell in the UK you will need you to create a new inventory listing for each new product that you want to sell there. Next, you will choose a customs broker through your carrier that will help you manage customs fees. Then, you will go about your product shipment as usual, except that you will need to add one additional stop to your shipment process. Your product will need to first be shipped to the chosen port to be cleared by customs, and then you will need to ship it to your FBA center to be sold to that particular marketplace.

If you want to sell overseas, you will have to go through this process with every single country that you want to sell in, in order to register and sell in each unique marketplace. This is not automatic, so you will have to manually process it all on your own. However, once it is done, the entire process is more or less the same from marketplace to marketplace. Furthermore, it is all still managed through your single Amazon Seller Central account.

Conclusion

Amazon FBA has been around since 2006, yet the opportunity of selling through Amazon FBA continues to thrive. To date, countless people have earned thousands, hundreds of thousands, and even millions by selling using the Amazon FBA platform. Creating sales, this way is a powerful opportunity for you to tap into eCommerce and earn a passive income online, regardless of how much or how little knowledge you have around running a business, or using tech to create an income.

When it comes to launching an Amazon FBA store, there is a simple seven-step process that you can follow to get your business out there. The first step is, as you know, launching your Amazon FBA account with Amazon Seller Central so that you can begin to access Amazon's tools and tap into their various features that are available to Amazon account holders. Without Amazon's Seller Central account, you will not be able to access any Amazon selling features, so this account is crucial.

The next six steps are oriented around choosing products, identifying suppliers, buying products, and marketing your products to your audience. On the issue of launching an Amazon FBA business, your entire role is to ensure that you have inventory in stock at the Amazon warehouse and then to market that inventory to your audience. You can market to people using paid advertisements, organic marketing strategies, and even word of mouth as an opportunity to get your name out there and have people purchasing your products.

If you choose to launch an Amazon FBA business, it is crucial that you follow the steps outlined in this book, in order to make sure that you generate a successful business through Amazon FBA. These steps have been organized in the exact order that you need to follow, therefore you generate traffic and grow your Amazon FBA business. If you do not follow these steps in order, you might find yourself missing important steps and paying the price in the end due to this very factor.

If you are just now launching your business, I strongly encourage you to start by identifying and marketing your brand on platforms like Instagram and Facebook, while you begin conducting all of the research for your business. The bigger that you can build your brand up in the beginning, the more momentum you will have to flow with right from the start. Remember, these are the earliest people who are going to buy from your business, and they are some of the most important. The more sales that you can generate early on, the more momentum you are going to gain, which means that you will gain even more traffic and even better search rankings on Amazon. It is well worth it to invest extra time in this part of the business to ensure that you are more likely to generate success in the end.

Lastly, if you have read *Amazon FBA* to help you launch your own Amazon FBA business and you feel that this book as supported you in generating success, I ask that you please review it on Amazon Kindle. Your honest feedback would be greatly appreciated.

Thank you and good luck with your Amazon FBA business!

Jim Work